250
Easy-to-Follow Vegetarian Recipes Cookbook for Beginners:

Healthy Vegetarian Cooking.

by

Noah White

Table of Contents

Main Meals..64

Drinks 125

Desserts 129

Introduction

A vegetarian diet is one of the healthy eating options that encourage you to eat fresh and healthy plant-based foods. Compared to non-vegetarian food, vegetarian food is high in fiber content and also lower in cholesterol and saturated fats. A study published by the University of Oxford (30 January 2013 in American Journal of Clinical Nutrition) shows that people following a vegetarian diet have a lower risk of heart disease, diabetes, obesity, osteoporosis, and in some cases, it reduces the risk of cancer compared to non-vegetarian people. There are endless varieties available in vegetarian food. Plant-based foods like fresh fruits, vegetables, beans, grains, and pulses are not only providing protein, omega-3, and fats but also a good source of other essential nutrients and minerals. If you want to lose body weight, then you have to eat low calorie good food. A vegetarian diet is a low calorie diet which not only reduces your weight but also keeps you healthy and strong.

Today most farming has shifted towards organic farming. The crops, vegetables, and fruits grown in organic farming are healthy and nutrient-rich foods grown without using harmful pesticides, fertilizers, growth hormones, and antibiotics, etc.

There are many reasons health-conscious people adopt a vegetarian lifestyle.. Non-vegetarians think that non-vegetarian foods are healthier than vegetarian food, but according to the study by Loma Linda University in California in 1958, vegetarian men and women live at least 9 to 6 years longer than fish and meat-eaters.

The book contains 250 healthy vegetarian recipes from breakfast, to main meals to desserts. All the recipes are well tested and written in an easily understandable form. Every recipe written in this book is healthy and perfectly balanced with proteins, fats, and carbs. You can easily make these recipes in your kitchen. The recipes written in this book are given with their exact preparation and cooking time. The nutritional values of each and every recipe are written at the end of the recipe. This helps you to know what you are getting after each meal. My goal here is to introduce you to a healthy vegetarian lifestyle and provide you with recipes that are tasty, healthy, and delicious vegetarian dishes. There are various types of books available on the market on this topic, thanks for choosing my book. I hope you enjoy all the healthy and delicious recipes written in this book.

Types of vegetarian

Vegetarians are divided into the following categories

1. **Vegans:** It is also known as a strict vegetarian diet. Most people fall in this category. Non-animal products such as vegetables, fruits, soy, grains, and nuts are allowed in this category. Vegans do not consume any animal foods such as meat, fish, chicken, and also avoid animal byproducts such as eggs, milk, yogurt, etc. Due to health reasons, some peoples go with strict vegans.
2. **Lacto Vegetarian:** People who come under this category strictly avoid meat, fish, chicken, and eggs but are allowed to consume dairy products such as milk, cheese, and yogurt.
3. **Ovo Vegetarian:** People who come in this category avoid meat, fish, chicken, and dairy products but eggs are allowed to be consumed under this category.
4. **Lacto-Ovo Vegetarian:** In this category meat and fish are strictly avoided but dairy products and eggs are consumed. This is one of the most common categories of vegetarian people.

The remaining categories like Pescatarian, Pollotarian, and Flexitarian are not technically considered as a vegetarian.

A vegetarian diet is healthier than non-vegetarian

There are various reasons which show that being vegetarian is one of the healthiest choices instead of non-vegetarian.

A vegetarian diet is a balanced diet

A wide range of plant-based foods are available on a vegetarian diet. Fresh vegetables and fruits are packed full of vitamins and nutrients. It is also rich in fiber, which helps to improve your digestive process and avoid constipation. Starchy foods like potatoes, cereals, pasta, rice, and bread are a good source of energy and contain nutrients like vitamin B, calcium, iron, and fiber.

Dairy products such as cheese, yogurts are the best sources of calcium, protein, and vitamins A and B12. Dairy alternative products such as soy, oat, and rice drinks are a rich source of calcium. Unsaturated fats such as sunflower oil, rapeseed oil, olive oil are the best alternatives over saturated fats like lard and butter. All fats are high in energy so limit fats in daily cooking and also limit salt, sugar, etc. Overall, the vegetarian diet is one of the most balanced diets.

Good for heart health

A vegetarian diet is low in saturated fats, high in fiber, vitamins, minerals, and essential nutrients. This will help you to keep your blood pressure level and cholesterol level stable. Omega-3 fatty acids are good for heart health, it keeps your heart healthy. In a vegetarian diet, soybean, flax seeds, canola oil, and walnut are the best source of plant-based omega-3 fatty acids. A vegetarian diet helps to lower the bad cholesterol (LDL) level and increase the good cholesterol (HDL) level. This will help to reduce heart-related problems and keep your heart healthy and strong.

Increased lifespan

A research study (published in JAMA internal medicine journal) conducted about a vegetarian diet proved that vegetarian people have a lowered risk of heart-related disease, cancer, and other chronic diseases compare to non-vegetarians. The study also proved that people who followed a vegetarian diet, lived 7 years more than meat-eaters; and those following a vegan diet lived for more than 15 years compared to meat-eaters. The study also showed that the risk of early death was lower in people following a vegetarian diet compared to non-vegetarians. Due to all these reasons, vegetarian people have lived a long and healthy life.

Reduces the risk of type-2 diabetes

To keep your blood sugar level stable, you have to choose low carb food in a vegetarian diet like legumes, whole grains, and nuts. The study published in PLOS Medicine Journal in June 2016, suggests that the reduction of meat and dairy products from daily diet and increase intake of vegetables, fruits, seeds, and nuts helps to reduce the risk of type-2 diabetes.

High in fiber

Vegetables and fruit are high in fiber which helps to improve your digestive system. Vegetarian foods are rich in water which also helps to maintain the liquid level in your body. Fiber-rich food also helps to improve your body's metabolism, in this process, toxins and other harmful chemicals are eliminated from your body. It also helps to reduce your excess body weight by controlling your food cravings The Department of health studies, University of Chicago, the USA published in April 2013 shows a high fiber intake will help to reduce the risk of colon cancer.

Important kitchen tools and equipment

Kitchen tools are useful for your daily cooking. They make your cooking process easy and also save you time and effort. Some of the essential kitchen tools and equipment are given below with their functions.

- **Knives:** One of the most useful kitchen tools to cut down your favorite vegetables into different shapes and sizes. It makes the cutting, chopping, and dicing process easy especially when you are cutting harder fruits and vegetables like onion, potatoes, and squashes.
- **Stockpots:** A stockpot is a wide pot having a flat bottomed surface especially used for making pho broth or vegetable soup.
- **Skillet:** This is used for sautéing, frying, baking, searing, roasting, and broiling your favorite vegetarian food. Preferably choose a non-stick skillet which makes your cooking and cleaning process easy.
- **Sheet pan:** This is a rectangular shaped nonstick baking sheet used for both baking and cooking your favorite food.
- **Metal strainer:** This is used to separate solids and liquids; a strainer can rinse beans and lentils and also be used to drain cooked foods like pasta and noodles.
- **Spoons, whisk, and spatulas:** All these accessories are available in wood, metal, and BPA free nylon materials. Metal accessories are not suitable for some of the nonstick pots. The accessories made from BPA free nylon are suitable in all conditions.
- **Chopping pad:** Choose a lightweight and large wooden chopping pad which fulfills all your chopping needs.
- **Mixing Bowls:** These bowls are used to perform most of the mixing tasks like mixing dry ingredients, making dough, mixing salads, and more.
- **Aluminum foil and parchment paper:** Aluminum foil can be used to wrap foods, cover baking surfaces, and wrap vegetables for grilling. Parchment paper is used especially when you are cooking in the oven. It is grease and moist resistance paper also used to cover a countertop while performing messy tasks.
- **Measuring tools:** The essential tools include measuring spoons from teaspoon to tablespoon, liquid measuring cups, and dry ingredient measuring cups.
- **Blender:** It helps to make sauces and dips. You can also use an immersion blender to blend your sauces in the cooking pot this will save you time and effort.

Essential tools

These tools are for those peoples who have a busy schedule and want to spend less time in the kitchen. All these tools make your daily cooking process easy.

- **Vegetable peeler:** This is a kitchen tool that comes with a sharp metal blade attached with handle. It is used to remove the hard surface of potatoes, carrots, cucumber, and fruits easily.

- **Cheese grater:** This tool is used for grating cheese, to create lemon and orange zest, also grate ginger and garlic instead of mincing.
- **Food Processor:** This is one of the most used kitchen gadgets and found in most kitchens. It helps to chop your vegetables, to make dough, slice, shred, grind, make a puree, citrus juice, and vegetable juice.
- **Garlic Press:** This tool is used to mince garlic cloves it extracts pulp and juice from garlic.
- **Mandolin slicer: This** is a handy kitchen gadget used for slicing fruits and vegetables, making French fries and salad. It is one of the great tools that makes your slicing and dicing job easy.
- **Rice cooker:** A rice cooker is used to cook rice, make oatmeal, steam your vegetables, and slow cook your soups, stews, and beans.

Balanced Vegetarian Dishes

When you completely switch to a vegetarian diet one question always in mind is can I get enough protein, and omega-3 from veggies? The answer is yes, you will find all these nutrients in vegetarian dishes.

- **Protein**

    It is one of the essential nutrients used to build and repair the tissues. It is also used to develop hormones, enzymes, and other chemicals that are required for overall body development. A single vegetable doesn't deliver full protein requirements. You have to combine these foods to meet the protein requirements. Soybeans are a protein-rich food which you can combine with peanut butter, tofu, tempeh, seitan, edamame beans, Greek yogurt, cooked lentils, cooked chickpeas, black beans, almonds, chia seeds, hemp seeds, quinoa, cottage cheese, and eggs. All these foods are sufficient to meet your daily protein requirements. Many people use tofu as a meat substitute. It not only supplies protein to your body but is also a good source of iron and calcium.

- **Omega-3**

    Omega-3 is a fatty acid good for your heart health. It fights depression and anxiety, and also improves eye health, reduces symptoms of metabolic syndrome, it is beneficial in Alzheimer's, can prevent cancer, and also improves bone and joint health. The best sources of Omega-3 fatty acids are fish. In a vegetarian diet high omega-3 includes,

    - **Chia seeds:** Chia seeds are enriched with ALA Omega-3 fatty acids and are a good source of fiber and protein. They helps to decrease blood triglyceride. They also help to increase the level of omega-3 fatty acids and good cholesterol (HDL).
    - **Flaxseeds:** Flaxseeds are a good source of omega-3 fatty acids. They are also enriched with protein, fiber, and magnesium. They also reduce your cholesterol level and maintain your blood pressure level.
    - **Walnuts:** Walnuts are a good source of healthy fats and omega-3 fatty acids. It helps to improve your brainpower and they are also effective with Alzheimer's condition. Walnuts also enriched with antioxidants which help to fight for oxidative damage into your body.
    - **Brussels sprouts:** Brussels sprouts are a good source of omega-3 fatty acids, high in nutrients, rich in antioxidants and also contain fiber, vitamin C, and vitamin K.
    - **Oils:** Soybean oil, flaxseed oil, walnut oil, canola oil, coconut oil, peanut oil, and sunflower oil are some healthy options used in a vegetarian diet. Fats provide more than 50 percent of the daily body energy needs. A moderate amount of unsaturated fats keeps you healthy.

Breakfast

High Protein Tofu Scramble

Cook time: 10 minutes | Serves: 2 | Per Serving: Calories 205, Carbs 3.5g, Fat 13.1g, Protein 20.3g

Ingredients:

- Extra-firm tofu – 8 oz., mash with a fork
- Soy milk – 1/3 cup
- Onion powder – ¼ tsp.
- Garlic powder – ½ tsp.
- Dijon mustard – 1 tsp.
- Paprika – ½ tsp.
- Turmeric – ½ tsp.
- Nutritional yeast – 2 tbsps.
- Butter – 1 tbsp.
- Salt – ¼ tsp.

Directions:

In a small bowl, mix together nutritional yeast, onion powder, garlic powder, mustard, paprika, turmeric, and salt. Add milk and whisk well. Heat butter in a pan over a medium heat. Add tofu to the pan and stir until lightly browned. Now add the nutritional yeast mixture to the pan and stir everything well and cook until the tofu has absorbed all the liquid. Serve.

Mini Kale Egg Muffins

Cook time: 20 minutes | Serves: 9 | Per Serving: Calories 42, Carbs 0.9g, Fat 2.2g, Protein 4.4g

Ingredients:

- Large Eggs – 4
- Sun-dried tomatoes – ¼ cup, chopped
- Kale – ½ cup, chopped
- Egg whites – ½ cup
- Pepper & salt, to taste

Directions:

Preheat the oven to 350 F. Spray muffin pan with cooking spray and set aside. In a mixing bowl, whisk eggs and egg whites. Add sun-dried tomatoes, kale, pepper, and salt and whisk well. Pour egg mixture into the prepared muffin pan and bake in a preheated oven for 20 minutes. Allow to cool for 10 minutes. Serve.

Healthy Oatmeal Cake

Cook time: 25 minutes | Serves: 8 | Per Serving: Calories 130, Carbs 18g, Fat 5g, Protein 3g

Ingredients:

- Eggs – 2
- Oats – 1 cup
- Butter – 1 tbsp.
- Yogurt – 3 tbsps.
- Baking powder – ½ tsp.
- Baking soda – ½ tsp.
- Cinnamon – 1 tsp.
- Vanilla– 1 tsp.
- Honey– 3 tbsps.
- Apple– 1, peeled & chopped

Directions:

Preheat the oven to 350 F. Add ¾ cup oats and remaining ingredients into the blender and blend until smooth. Add remaining oats and mix well. Pour batter into the parchment-lined baking pan and bake in a preheated oven for 20-30 minutes. Slice and serve.

Baked Pumpkin Oatmeal

Cook time: 35 minutes | Serves: 6 | Per Serving: Calories 205, Carbs 40g, Fat 3g, Protein 5g

Ingredients:

- Egg – 1
- Ground cloves – 1/8 tsp.
- Allspice – ¼ tsp.
- Ground ginger – ¼ tsp.
- Ground cinnamon – 1 ½ tsps.
- Baking powder – 1 tsp.
- Rolled oats – 2 cups
- Apple – 1, diced
- Vanilla – 1 tsp.
- Maple syrup – ¼ cup
- Unsweetened almond milk – 11/2 cups
- Unsweetened pumpkin puree – 1 cup
- For topping:
- Ground cinnamon – ¾ tsp.
- Sugar – 1 ½ tbsps.

Directions:

Preheat the oven to 350 F. Spray 9*9-inch baking dish with cooking spray and set aside. In a large mixing bowl, whisk together egg, vanilla, milk, and pumpkin puree. Add remaining ingredients except for topping ingredients and stir well. Pour mixture into the prepared dish. Mix together sugar and cinnamon and sprinkle on top of the oatmeal mixture. Bake oatmeal in a preheated oven for 30-35 minutes. Allow to cool for 10 minutes. Serve.

Easy & Tasty Breakfast Potatoes

Cook time: 25 minutes | Serves: 2 | Per Serving: Calories 220, Carbs 35.2g, Fat 7.2g, Protein 4g

Ingredients:

- Potatoes – 1 lb., peeled & diced
- Paprika – ½ tsp.
- Garlic powder – ½ tsp.
- Italian seasoning – 2 tsps.
- Olive oil – 1 tbsp.
- Black pepper – 1/8 tsp.
- Salt – ½ tsp.

Directions:

Preheat the oven to 400 F. Add all ingredients into the mixing bowl and mix well. Place potatoes onto a parchment-lined baking sheet and bake in a preheated oven for 25-30 minutes or until lightly golden brown. Serve.

Egg Mixed Veggie Muffins

Cook time: 22 minutes | Serves: 12 | Per Serving: Calories 145, Carbs 7g, Fat 8g, Protein 10g

Ingredients:

- Large eggs – 12
- Parmesan cheese – ¼ cup, grated
- Cheddar cheese – 1 cup, shredded
- Onion – 3 tbsps., minced
- Mustard powder – ½ tsp.
- Milk – ¼ cup
- Olive oil – 1 tsp.
- Mixed vegetables – 3 cups, chopped
- Black pepper– ½ tsp.
- Salt– ½ tsp.

Directions:

Preheat the oven to 350 F. Spray muffin pan with cooking spray and set aside. Heat oil in a pan over a medium heat. Add mixed vegetables to the pan and sauté until tender. Remove pan from heat and let it cool. In a mixing bowl, whisk eggs, seasonings, and milk. Add sautéed vegetables, onion, and cheeses and whisk well. Pour egg mixture into the prepared muffin pan and bake for 22-25 minutes. Allow to cool completely. Serve.

Sweet Potato Hash

Cook time: 1 hour 5 minutes | Serves: 6 | Per Serving: Calories 296, Carbs 45g, Fat 11g, Protein 3g

Ingredients:

- Sweet potatoes – 6 cups, peeled and diced
- Paprika – ½ tsp.
- Pepper – ½ tsp.
- Thyme – 1 tsp.
- Onion powder – 1 tsp.
- Onion – 1, diced
- Garlic cloves – 4, minced
- Olive oil – 1/3 cup
- Garlic powder – 1 tbsp.
- Salt – 2 tsps.

Directions:

Preheat the oven to 450 F. Add sweet potatoes to a casserole dish and sprinkle with garlic powder, pepper, paprika, thyme, onion powder, and salt. Drizzle oil over sweet potatoes and toss well. Roast in preheated oven for 55-65 minutes. Stir 3-4 times. Heat 1 tablespoon of olive oil in a pan over medium heat. Add onion and garlic and sauté for 12-15 minutes. Once sweet potatoes are cooked then remove from oven. Add onion and garlic mixture to the sweet potatoes and stir well. Serve.

Potato Egg Casserole

Cook time: 35 minutes | Serves: 6 | Per Serving: Calories 178, Carbs 14.4g, Fat 9.7g, Protein 9.1g

Ingredients:

- Eggs – 5
- Cheddar cheese – ½ cup, shredded
- Medium potatoes – 2, diced into ½-inch cubes
- Green bell pepper – 1, diced
- Onion – 1, chopped
- Olive oil – 1 tbsp.
- Black pepper – ¾ tsp.
- Salt – ¾ tsp.

Directions:

Preheat the oven to 350 F. Spray 9*9-inch casserole dish with cooking spray and set aside. Heat olive oil in a large pan over a medium heat. Add onion and sauté for 1 minute. Add potatoes, bell peppers, ½ tsp black pepper, and ½tsp salt and sauté for 4 minutes more or until onions are softened. Transfer sautéed vegetables to the prepared casserole dish and spread evenly. In a bowl, whisk eggs, and remaining pepper and salt. Pour egg mixture into the casserole dish and sprinkle cheddar cheese on top. Bake in a preheated oven for 35-40 minutes. Serve.

Quinoa Broccoli Cheese Muffins

Cook time: 20 minutes | Serves: 12 | Per Serving: Calories 112, Carbs 7g, Fat 6g, Protein 7g

Ingredients:

- Eggs – 8
- Mozzarella cheese – ¾ cup, shredded
- Broccoli florets – 2 cups, chopped
- Onion – 1, grated
- Quinoa – 1 ½ cups, cooked
- Pepper & salt, to taste

Directions:

Preheat the oven to 400 F. Spray muffin pan with cooking spray and set aside. In a mixing bowl, mix cooked quinoa, broccoli, cheese, onion, pepper, and salt. In a separate bowl, whisk eggs until light. Pour egg into the egg mixture and mix well. Pour quinoa egg mixture into the prepared muffin pan and bake for 20 minutes. Let it cool for 5-10 minutes. Serve.

Perfect Mocha Oats

Cook time: 5 minutes | Serves: 1 | Per Serving: Calories 146, Carbs 19.3g, Fat 6.1g, Protein 5.9g

Ingredients:

- Rolled oats – ¼ cup
- Cocoa powder – 1 tbsp.
- Unsweetened almond milk – ½ cup
- Brewed coffee – ¾ cup
- Chia seeds – 1 tbsp.

Directions:

Add all ingredients into the mason jar and mix well. Place jar in the fridge for 4 hours. Stir well and serve.

Peanut Butter Oats

Cook time: 5 minutes | Serves: 2 | Per Serving: Calories 450, Carbs 60g, Fat 20g, Protein 13g

Ingredients:

- Cinnamon – ½ tsp.
- Unsweetened almond milk – 1 cup
- Large ripe bananas – 2
- Rolled oats – ¾ cup
- Peanut butter – ¼ cup

Directions:

Add bananas into the large bowl and mash until smooth. Add remaining ingredients and mix well. Transfer mixture into a glass mason jar. Seal jar with lid and place in the fridge overnight. Serve.

Easy Omelette Muffins

Cook time: 20 minutes | Serves: 12 | Per Serving: Calories 95, Carbs 1g, Fat 6g, Protein 7g

Ingredients:

- Eggs – 8
- Baby spinach – ½ cup, chopped
- Bell peppers – 1 cup, diced
- Cheddar cheese – 1 cup, shredded
- Milk – ½ cup
- Pepper & salt, to taste

Directions:

Preheat the oven to 350 F. Spray muffin pan with cooking spray and set aside. In a mixing bowl, whisk eggs and milk. Stir in spinach, bell peppers, cheese, pepper, and salt. Pour egg mixture into the prepared muffin pan and bake in a preheated oven for 20-25 minutes. Allow to cool for 5-10 minutes. Serve.

Blueberry Oats

Cook time: 7 hours | Serves: 6 | Per Serving: Calories 155, Carbs 26g, Fat 4g, Protein 4g

Ingredients:

- Steel-cut oats – 1 cup
- Vanilla – 1 tsp.
- Water – 5 cups
- Quinoa – ½ cup, rinsed
- Blueberries – 1 cup
- Maple syrup – 2 tbsps.
- Coconut oil – 1 tbsp., melted
- Lemon zest – 1 tbsp.
- Salt – ¼ tsp.

Directions:

Spray slow cooker with cooking spray. Add all ingredients into the slow cooker and stir well. Cover slow cooker with lid and cook on low for 7 hours. Serve.

Smooth Sweet Potato Mash

Cook time: 20 minutes | Serves: 4 | Per Serving: Calories 255, Carbs 56g, Fat 1g, Protein 7g

Ingredients:

- Sweet potato – 2 lbs., peel and diced
- Maple syrup – 2 tbsps.
- Unsweetened almond milk – ¼ cup

- Garlic powder – 1 tsp.
- Nutritional yeast – 2 tbsps.
- Pepper & salt, to taste

Directions:

Boil sweet potatoes for 20-25 minutes or until softened. Drain well and transfer in a large bowl. Add remaining ingredients into the bowl. Mash sweet potatoes until smooth. Season with pepper and salt. Serve.

Coconut Pineapple Oats

Cook time: 5 minutes │Serves: 1 │ Per Serving: Calories 283, Carbs 41.6g, Fat 8.4g, Protein 12.4g

Ingredients:

- Rolled oats – 1/3 cup
- Shredded unsweetened coconut – 1 tbsp.
- Pineapple chunks – 4 tbsps.
- Chia seeds – 2 tsps.
- Unsweetened almond milk – 1/3 cup
- Plain Greek yogurt – 1/3 cup

Directions:

Add all ingredients into the mason jar and mix well. Place jar in the fridge overnight. Stir well and serve.

Italian Frittata

Cook time: 30 minutes │Serves: 4 │ Per Serving: Calories 325, Carbs 3.5g, Fat 23g, Protein 25g

Ingredients:

- Eggs – 8
- Zucchini – 2, chopped and cooked
- Fresh parsley – 1 tbsp, chopped
- Parmesan cheese – 3 tbsps., grated
- Pepper & salt, to taste

Directions:

Grease baking dish and set aside. Preheat the oven to 350 F. In a mixing bowl, whisk eggs with pepper and salt. Add parsley, cheese, and zucchini and stir well. Pour egg mixture into the prepared baking dish and Bake for 20 minutes. Serve.

Broccoli Egg Bake

Cook time: 30 minutes │Serves: 12 │ Per Serving: Calories 135, Carbs 3.1g, Fat 10g, Protein 10g

Ingredients:

- Eggs – 12
- Onion – 1, diced
- Milk – 1 cup
- Cheddar cheese – 1 1/2 cups, shredded
- Broccoli florets – 2 cups, chopped
- Pepper & salt, to taste

Directions:

Grease a 9*13-inch baking dish and set aside. Preheat the oven to 390 F. In a large bowl, whisk eggs with milk, pepper, and salt. Add cheese, broccoli, and onion and stir well. Pour egg mixture into the prepared baking dish and bake for 30 minutes. Serve.

Zucchini Kale Bake

Cook time: 30 minutes | Serves: 4 | Per Serving: Calories 330, Carbs 11g, Fat 23g, Protein 20g

Ingredients:

- Eggs – 6
- Dill – 1/2 tsp.
- Oregano – 1/2 tsp.
- Basil – 1/2 tsp.
- Baking powder – 1/2 tsp.
- Almond flour – 1/2 cup
- Cheddar cheese – 1 cup, shredded
- Kale – 1 cup, chopped
- Onion – 1, chopped
- Zucchini – 1 cup, shredded and squeezed out all liquid
- Milk – 1/2 cup
- Salt – 1/4 tsp.

Directions:

Grease 9*9-inch baking dish and set aside. Preheat the oven to 375 F. In a large bowl, whisk eggs with milk. Add remaining ingredients and stir until well combined. Pour egg mixture into the prepared dish and bake for 35 minutes. Serve.

Baked Berry Oatmeal

Cook time: 20 minutes | Serves: 4 | Per Serving: Calories 460, Carbs 80g, Fat 8g, Protein 15g

Ingredients:

- Egg – 1
- Maple syrup – 1/4 cup
- Milk – 1 1/2 cups
- Baking powder – 1 1/2 tsps.
- Old fashioned oats – 2 cups

- Blueberries – 1 cup
- Blackberries – 1/2 cup
- Strawberries – 1/2 cup, sliced
- Salt – 1/2 tsp.

Directions:

Grease baking dish and set aside. Preheat the oven to 375 F. In a mixing bowl, mix together oats, salt, and baking powder. Add vanilla, egg, maple syrup, and milk and stir well. Add berries and stir well. Pour mixture into the baking dish and bake for 20 minutes. Serve.

Nutritious Overnight Strawberry Oats

Cook time: 5 minutes | Serves: 3 | Per Serving: Calories 304, Carbs 42.5g, Fat 7.8g, Protein 15.2g

Ingredients:

- Old-fashioned oats – 1 ½ cups
- Strawberries – ¾ cup, diced
- Strawberry Greek yogurt – 1 cup
- Chia seeds – 2 tbsps.
- Milk – 1 ½ cups

Directions:

Add all ingredients into the mixing bowl and mix well. Pour into the three mason jars. Place jars in the fridge for overnight. Serve.

Egg Kale Muffins

Cook time: 30 minutes | Serves: 8 | Per Serving: Calories 60, Carbs 2g, Fat 3.6g, Protein 5g

Ingredients:

- Eggs – 6
- Kale – 1 cup, chopped
- Milk – 1/2 cup
- Chives – 1/4 cup, chopped
- Pepper & salt, to taste

Directions:

Spray muffin pan with cooking spray and set aside. Preheat the oven to 350 F. Add all ingredients into the mixing bowl and whisk well. Pour mixture into the prepared muffin pan and bake for 30 minutes. Serve.

Asparagus Quiche

Cook time: 60 minutes | Serves: 6 | Per Serving: Calories 226, Carbs 6g, Fat 18g, Protein 12g

Ingredients:

- Eggs – 5, beaten
- Almond milk – 1 cup
- Thyme – 1/4 tsp.
- Asparagus spears – 15, cut ends then cut asparagus in half
- Swiss cheese – 1 cup, shredded
- White pepper – 1/4 tsp.
- Salt – 1/4 tsp.

Directions:

Grease baking pan and set aside. Preheat the oven to 350 F. In a bowl, whisk together eggs, thyme, white pepper, almond milk, and salt. Arrange asparagus in a baking pan then pour egg mixture over asparagus. Sprinkle with cheese. Bake for 60 minutes. Serve.

Vegetable Quiche Cups

Cook time: 20 minutes | Serves: 12 | Per Serving: Calories 75, Carbs 2g, Fat 5g, Protein 6g

Ingredients:

- Eggs – 8
- Onion – 1/4 cup, chopped
- Mushroom – 1/4 cup, diced
- Bell pepper – 1/4 cup, diced
- Cheddar cheese – 3/4 cup, shredded
- Frozen spinach – 10 oz, chopped

Directions:

Spray muffin pan with cooking spray and set aside. Preheat the oven to 375 F. Add all ingredients into the mixing bowl and beat until combine. Pour egg mixture into the prepared muffin pan and bake for 20 minutes. Serve.

Delicious Mushroom Frittata

Cook time: 20 minutes | Serves: 2 | Per Serving: Calories 575, Carbs 9.3g, Fat 48g, Protein 28.9g

Ingredients:

- Eggs – 6
- Butter – 2 oz
- Mushrooms – 5 oz., sliced
- Feta cheese – 4 oz., crumbled
- Scallions – 2 oz., chopped
- Fresh spinach – 3 oz.
- Pepper & salt, to taste

Directions:

Spray a baking dish with cooking spray and set aside. Preheat the oven to 350 F. In a bowl, whisk eggs, cheese, pepper, and salt. Melt butter in a pan over medium heat. Add mushrooms and scallions and sauté for 5-10 minutes. Add spinach and sauté for 2 minutes. Transfer mushroom mixture into the baking dish. Pour egg mixture over the mushroom mixture and bake for 20 minutes. Serve.

Easy & Delicious Oat Breakfast Smoothie

Cook time: 5 minutes | Serves: 4 | Per Serving: Calories 161, Carbs 29.9g, Fat 4.3g, Protein 3g

Ingredients:

- Rolled oats – ¼ cup
- Chia seeds – 1 tsp.
- Almond butter – 1 tbsp.
- Almond milk – 2 cups
- Vanilla – ½ tsp.
- Cardamom – 1/8 tsp.
- Ground ginger – ¼ tsp.
- Ground cinnamon – ½ tsp.
- Bananas – 2
- Large apple – 1, peeled, cored, & diced

Directions:

Add all ingredients into the blender and blend until smooth and creamy. Serve.

Snacks

Crunchy Roasted Chickpeas

Cook time: 30 minutes | Serves: 4 | Per Serving: Calories 159, Carbs 24.5g, Fat 4.8g, Protein 5.4g

Ingredients:

- Can chickpeas – 15 oz, drained & rinsed
- Ground cumin – 1/2 tsp.
- Smoked paprika – 1 tsp.
- Olive oil – 1 tbsp.
- Pepper – ¼ tsp.
- Salt – 1 tsp.

Directions:

Preheat the oven to 400 F. Place chickpeas on a parchment-lined baking sheet and bake in preheated oven for 15 minutes. Remove chickpeas from the oven and mix with oil and spices. Return chickpeas to the oven and bake for 15 minutes more or until crispy. Remove chickpeas from the oven and let them cool completely. Serve.

Toasted Pecans

Cook time: 45 minutes | Serves: 16 | Per Serving: Calories 241, Carbs 4g, Fat 25g, Protein 3g

Ingredients:

- Raw pecans – 4 cups
- Butter – ½ cup, melted
- Kosher salt – 2 tsps.

Directions:

Preheat the oven to 275 F. Toss pecans with melted butter and spread on a parchment-lined baking sheet. Toast pecans in preheated oven for 45 minutes. Stir after every 15 minutes. Once done, then remove from the oven and let them cool completely. Season with salt and serve.

Sweet & Spicy Nuts

Cook time: 20 minutes | Serves: 16 | Per Serving: Calories 238, Carbs 9g, Fat 21.7g, Protein 5.6g

Ingredients:

- Mixed nuts – 4 cups
- Maple syrup – 1 tbsp.
- Chili powder – 1 tsp.
- Butter – 2 tbsps., melted
- Salt – 1 ½ tsps.

Directions:

Preheat the oven to 300 F. In a mixing bowl, mix together melted butter, maple syrup, chili powder, and salt. Add mixed nuts and toss to coat. Spread nuts onto the parchment-lined baking sheet and bake in preheated oven for 15-20 minutes. Serve.

Sweet & Spicy Cashews

Cook time: 10 minutes | Serves: 8 | Per Serving: Calories 280, Carbs 24.6g, Fat 18.7g, Protein 7.8g

Ingredients:

- Raw cashew nuts – 12 oz.
- Coconut sugar – 2 tbsps.
- Chili powder – 1 tsp.
- Honey – ¼ cup
- Sea salt – 1 ½ tsps.

Directions:

Preheat the oven to 325 F. Line baking sheet with parchment paper and set aside. In a microwave-safe bowl, stir together honey and chili powder and microwave for 10-15 seconds. Add cashews to the honey mixture and toss to coat. Spread cashews on a prepared baking sheet and roast in a preheated oven for 10-15 minutes. Stir after every 5 minutes. Remove cashews from the oven and let them cool for 5 minutes. Mix together coconut sugar and salt and sprinkle over cashews. Serve.

Spicy Almonds

Cook time: 20 minutes | Serves: 6 | Per Serving: Calories 230, Carbs 8.9g, Fat 19.9g, Protein 7.8g

Ingredients:

- Raw almonds – 1 ½ cups
- Ground cayenne – ½ tsp.
- Onion powder – ¼ tsp.
- Dried basil – ¼ tsp.
- Garlic powder – ½ tsp.
- Cumin – ½ tsp.
- Chili powder – 1 ½ tsps.
- Worcestershire sauce – 2 tsps.
- Butter – 2 tbsps., melted
- Sea salt – ½ tsp.

Directions:

Preheat the oven to 350 F. In a large mixing bowl, whisk melted butter, cayenne, onion powder, basil, garlic powder, cumin, chili powder, and Worcestershire sauce. Add almonds and toss to coat. Spread almonds on a parchment-lined baking sheet and bake for 18-20 minutes. Stir 2-3 times. Remove from the oven and let them cool for 5-10 minutes. Season with salt and serve.

Roasted Sweet Potatoes

Cook time: 45 minutes | Serves: 6 | Per Serving: Calories 220, Carbs 40g, Fat 5g, Protein 2g

Ingredients:

- Sweet potatoes – 2 lbs, peel and cut into ½-inch cubes
- Onion powder – ½ tsp.
- Garlic powder – ½ tsp.
- Chili powder – ½ tsp.
- Cinnamon – ½ tsp.
- Olive oil – 2 tbsps.
- Pepper & salt, to taste

Directions:

Preheat the oven to 400 F. Line baking sheet with parchment paper and set aside. Spread sweet potato on a prepared baking sheet. Drizzle with oil and season with spices. Toss to coat. Roast in preheated oven for 40-45 minutes. Stir halfway through. Season with salt. Serve.

Healthy Carrot Fries

Cook time: 25 minutes | Serves: 4 | Per Serving: Calories 76, Carbs 6g, Fat 5g, Protein 0.7g

Ingredients:

- Medium carrots – 4, peel and cut into the shape of fries
- Cumin powder – 1 tsp.
- Paprika – ½ tbsp.
- Olive oil – 1 ½ tbsps.
- Salt – ½ tsp.

Directions:

Preheat the oven to 450 F. Add carrots, cumin powder, paprika, oil, and salt into the large bowl and toss well. Spread carrot fries on a baking sheet and bake for 10 minutes. Stir and bake for 15 minutes more. Serve.

Sweet Potato Croquettes

Cook time: 60 minutes | Serves: 6 | Per Serving: Calories 110, Carbs 23g, Fat 1g, Protein 2g

Ingredients:

- Quinoa – 2 cups, cooked
- Italian seasoning – 2 tsps.
- Garlic clove – 1, minced
- Celery – ¼ cup, diced
- Scallions – ¼ cup, chopped
- Parsley – ¼ cup, chopped

- Flour – ¼ cup
- Sweet potatoes – 2 cups, mashed
- Pepper & salt, to taste

Directions:

Preheat the oven to 375 F. Spray a baking sheet with cooking spray and set aside. Add all ingredients into the large bowl and mix well. Make 1-inch croquettes from mixture and place on a baking sheet. Bake croquettes for 1 hour. Serve.

Roasted Garlic Olives

Cook time: 5 minutes | Serves: 4 | Per Serving: Calories 140, Carbs 5g, Fat 14g, Protein 0.7g

Ingredients:

- Olives – 2 cups
- Crushed red pepper – 1/2 tsp.
- Garlic – 2 tsps., minced
- Olive oil – 2 tbsps.
- Dried fennel seeds – 1/2 tsp.
- Dried oregano – 1/2 tsp.
- Pepper & salt, to taste

Directions:

Add olives and remaining ingredients into the mixing bowl and mix well. Add olives into the air fryer basket and air fry at 300 F for 5 minutes. Serve.

Tasty Cauliflower Bites

Cook time: 15 minutes | Serves: 4 | Per Serving: Calories 65, Carbs 7g, Fat 0g, Protein 2.5g

Ingredients:

- Cauliflower florets – 1 lb.
- Sesame seeds – 1 tsp.
- Ground coriander – 1 tsp.
- Dried rosemary – 1/2 tsp.
- Garlic powder – 1 1/2 tsps.
- Olive oil – 1 tbsp.
- Pepper & salt, to taste

Directions:

Add cauliflower florets and remaining ingredients into the large bowl and toss well. Spread cauliflower florets on baking sheet and bake for 400 F for 15 minutes. Serve.

Spicy Walnuts

Cook time: 5 minutes | Serves: 6 | Per Serving: Calories 264, Carbs 4g, Fat 24g, Protein 10g

Ingredients:

- Walnuts – 2 cups
- Olive oil – 1 tsp.
- Chili powder – 1/4 tsp.
- Pepper & salt, to taste

Directions:

Add walnuts, chili powder, oil, pepper, and salt into the mixing bowl and toss well. Add walnuts into the air fryer basket and air fry at 320 for 5 minutes. Serve.

Sweet Potato Bites

Cook time: 15 minutes | Serves: 2 | Per Serving: Calories 295, Carbs 43g, Fat 14g, Protein 3g

Ingredients:

- Sweet potato – 2, diced into 1-inch cubes
- Honey – 2 tbsps.
- Red chili flakes – 1 tsp.
- Fresh parsley – 1/2 cup, chopped
- Cinnamon – 1 1/2 tsps.
- Olive oil – 2 tbsps.

Directions:

Add all ingredients into the mixing bowl and mix well. Add sweet potato cubes into the air fryer basket and air fry at 350 F for 15 minutes. Shake basket halfway through. Serve.

Herb Mushrooms

Cook time: 14 minutes | Serves: 4 | Per Serving: Calories 25, Carbs 4g, Fat 0.5g, Protein 3.5g

Ingredients:

- Mushroom caps – 1 lb.
- Basil – 1 tbsp., minced
- Garlic clove – 1, minced
- Vinegar – 1/2 tbsp.
- Ground coriander – 1/2 tsp.
- Rosemary –, chopped 1 tsp.
- Pepper & salt, to taste

Directions:

Add all ingredients into the bowl and toss well. Add mushrooms into the air fryer basket and air fry at 350 F for 14 minutes. Shake basket halfway through. Serve.

Crispy Cauliflower Florets

Cook time: 15 minutes │Serves: 5 │ Per Serving: Calories 105, Carbs 6g, Fat 8.5g, Protein 2.4g

Ingredients:

- Medium cauliflower head – 1, cut into florets
- Garlic – 1 tbsp., minced
- Olive oil – 3 tbsps.
- Old bay seasoning – 1/2 tsp.
- Paprika – 1/4 tsp.
- Pepper & salt, to taste

Directions:

In a mixing bowl, toss cauliflower with remaining ingredients. Add cauliflower florets into the air fryer basket and air fry at 400 F for 15 minutes. Toss twice. Serve.

Easy Roasted Brussels sprouts

Cook time: 35 minutes │Serves: 6 │ Per Serving: Calories 86, Carbs 3g, Fat 8.5g, Protein 1g

Ingredients:

- Brussels sprouts – 2 cups, halved
- Olive oil – 1/4 cup
- Cayenne pepper – 1/4 tsp.
- Garlic powder – 1/4 tsp.
- Salt – 1/4 tsp.

Directions:

Preheat the oven to 400 F. Add all ingredients into the large bowl and toss well. Transfer Brussels sprouts on a baking sheet and roast in preheated oven for 30-35 minutes. Stir halfway through. Serve.

Tasty Potato Wedges

Cook time: 15 minutes │Serves: 4 │ Per Serving: Calories 120, Carbs 16g, Fat 5g, Protein 2g

Ingredients:

- Medium potatoes – 2, cut into wedges
- Cayenne pepper – 1/8 tsp.
- Garlic powder – 1/4 tsp.
- Paprika – 1/2 tsp.
- Olive oil – 1 1/2 tbsps.

- Pepper – 1/4 tsp.
- Sea salt – 1 tsp.

Directions:

Soak potato wedges in water for 30 minutes. Drain well and pat dry with a paper towel. In a bowl, toss potato wedges with remaining ingredients. Arrange potato wedges in the air fryer basket and air fry at 400 F for 15 minutes. Serve.

Parmesan Potatoes

Cook time: 45 minutes │Serves: 4 │ Per Serving: Calories 375, Carbs 45g, Fat 19g, Protein 8.5g

Ingredients:

- Potatoes – 5, cut into wedges
- Lemon juice – 2 tbsps.
- Olive oil – 1/3 cup
- Garlic cloves – 2, minced
- Thyme sprigs – 2
- Parmesan cheese – 1/2 cup, grated
- Pepper & salt, to taste

Directions:

Preheat the oven to 325 F. Grease a 9*13-inch baking dish and set aside. Add potato wedges into the baking dish. Mix together lemon juice, oil, garlic, thyme, cheese, pepper, and salt and pour over potatoes and toss well. Bake for 45 minutes. Serve.

Cheese Broccoli Fritters

Cook time: 30 minutes │Serves: 4 │ Per Serving: Calories 325, Carbs 7.5g, Fat 25g, Protein 20g

Ingredients:

- Broccoli florets – 3 cups, steam & chopped
- Cheddar cheese – 2 cups, shredded
- Almond flour – 1/4 cup
- Eggs – 2, lightly beaten
- Garlic cloves – 2, minced
- Pepper & salt, to taste

Directions:

Preheat the oven to 375 F. Add all ingredients into the large bowl and mix until well combined. Make patties from broccoli mixture and place on a parchment-lined baking sheet and bake for 15 minutes. Turn patties and bake for 15 minutes more. Serve.

Yummy Ranch Potatoes

Cook time: 20 minutes | Serves: 2 | Per Serving: Calories 100, Carbs 14g, Fat 3g, Protein 3g

Ingredients:

- Baby potatoes – 1/2 lb, wash and cut in half
- Olive oil – 1/2 tbsp
- Dill – 1/4 tsp.
- Chives – 1/4 tsp.
- Paprika – 1/4 tsp.
- Onion powder – 1/4 tsp.
- Garlic powder – 1/4 tsp.
- Parsley – 1/4 tsp.
- Salt

Directions:

Add all ingredients into the mixing bowl and toss well. Spread potatoes in air fryer basket and air fry at 400 F for 20 minutes. Serve.

Parmesan Zucchini Patties

Cook time: 25 minutes | Serves: 6 | Per Serving: Calories 65, Carbs 8g, Fat 2.5g, Protein 3.7g

Ingredients:

- Zucchini – 1 cup, shredded and squeeze out all liquid
- Onion – 2 tbsps., minced
- Egg – 1, lightly beaten
- Red pepper flakes – 1/4 tsp.
- Parmesan cheese – 1/4 cup, grated
- Dijon mustard – 1/2 tbsp.
- Mayonnaise – 1/2 tbsp.
- breadcrumbs – 1/2 cup
- Pepper & salt, to taste

Directions:

Add all ingredients into the bowl and mix until well combined. Make small patties from the zucchini mixture and place into the air fryer basket and air fry at 400 F for 25 minutes. Serve.

Simple Sweet Potato Fries

Cook time: 16 minutes | Serves: 2 | Per Serving: Calories 235, Carbs 40g, Fat 7g, Protein 2g

Ingredients:

- Sweet potatoes – 2, peeled and cut into fries shape
- Chili powder – 1/4 tsp.

- Olive oil – 1 tbsp.
- Salt

Directions:

In a large bowl, add sweet potato fries, chili powder, olive oil, and salt and toss until well coated. Add sweet potato fries into the air fryer basket and air fry at 380 F for 16 minutes. Serve.

Cheesy Brussels sprouts

Cook time: 12 minutes | Serves: 4 | Per Serving: Calories 95, Carbs 10g, Fat 5g, Protein 5g

Ingredients:

- Brussels sprouts – 1 lb, cut stems and halved
- Parmesan cheese – 1/4 cup, grated
- Olive oil – 1 tbsp.
- Pepper & salt, to taste

Directions:

Toss Brussels sprouts, oil, pepper, and salt into the mixing bowl. Transfer Brussels sprouts into the air fryer basket and air fry at 350 F for 12 minutes. Sprinkle with cheese and serve.

BBQ Seasoned Chickpeas

Cook time: 12 minutes | Serves: 4 | Per Serving: Calories 155, Carbs 25g, Fat 4.5g, Protein 5.1g

Ingredients:

- Can chickpeas – 14 oz, rinsed, drained and pat dry
- Olive oil – 1 tbsp.
- Dry mustard – 1/2 tsp.
- Garlic powder – 1/2 tsp.
- Brown sugar – 1 tsp.
- Paprika – 1 1/2 tsp.
- Pepper – 1/4 tsp.
- Salt – 1/2 tsp.

Directions:

Add chickpeas into the mixing bowl and toss with remaining ingredients. Spread chickpeas into the air fryer basket and air fry at 375 F for 12 minutes. Serve.

Spicy Okra

Cook time: 15 minutes | Serves: 4 | Per Serving: Calories 105, Carbs 8g, Fat 7g, Protein 2g

Ingredients:

- Fresh okra – 1 lb., cut into 3/4-inch pieces

- Paprika – 1 tsp.
- Chili powder – 1/4 tsp.
- Olive oil – 2 tbsps.
- Salt

Directions:

Preheat the oven to 390 F. Add okra, chili powder, paprika, oil, and salt into the bowl and toss well. Spread okra on a roasting pan and bake for 15 minutes. Serve.

Air Fried Cashew

Cook time: 10 minutes | Serves: 4 | Per Serving: Calories 350, Carbs 19g, Fat 25g, Protein 9g

Ingredients:

- Cashews – 1 2/3 cups
- Olive oil – 1 tsp.
- Red chili powder – 1 tsp.
- Coriander powder – 1 tsp.
- Pepper – 1/2 tsp.
- Salt – 1/2 tsp.

Directions:

Add all ingredients into the mixing bowl and toss well. Add cashews into the air fryer basket and air fry at 250 F for 10 minutes. Serve.

Salads

Mediterranean Chickpea Salad

Cook time: 5 minutes | Serves: 3 | Per Serving: Calories 159, Carbs 27g, Fat 3g, Protein 8g

Ingredients:

- Can chickpeas – 15 oz.
- Fresh parsley – 1 tbsp. , chopped
- Lemon juice – 1
- Onion – 2 tbsps., chopped
- Red pepper – ½, chopped
- Tomato – 1, chopped
- Cucumber – 1, chopped
- Kosher salt – 1 tsp.

Directions:

In a mixing bowl, mix together chickpeas, cucumber, tomatoes, red pepper, and onion. In a small bowl, mix together lemon juice, parsley, salt, and pour over salad and mix well. Serve.

Corn Cabbage Salad

Cook time: 5 minutes | Serves: 4 | Per Serving: Calories 173, Carbs 17g, Fat 12g, Protein 3g

Ingredients:

- Cabbage – 1 ½ lbs., sliced thinly
- Olive oil – 3 tbsps.
- Vinegar – 1 1/2 tbsps.
- Dill – 1/3 cup, chopped
- Corn – 1 cup
- Cucumber – ½, sliced
- Pepper – ½ tsp.
- Salt – ½ tsp.

Directions:

Add all ingredients into the mixing bowl and mix everything well. Serve.

Avocado Corn Tomato Salad

Cook time: 5 minutes | Serves: 4 | Per Serving: Calories 208, Carbs 19g, Fat 15g, Protein 4g

Ingredients:

- Corn – 1 ½ cups
- Avocado – 1, diced
- Cherry tomatoes – 2 cups, halved

- Romaine lettuce – 1 cup, chopped
- Fresh cilantro – 2 tbsps., chopped
- Fresh lime juice – 1 tbsp.
- Onion – 2 tbsps., chopped
- Pepper – ¼ tsp.
- Salt– ¼ tsp.

Directions:

In a mixing bowl, mix together lettuce, corn, cherry tomatoes, avocados, and onion. In a small bowl, mix together oil, lime juice, cilantro, pepper, and salt and pour over salad. Mix well and serve.

Eastern Bean Salad

Cook time: 5 minutes | Serves: 5 | Per Serving: Calories 85, Carbs 7g, Fat 6g, Protein 1g

Ingredients:

- Cucumber – 1, chopped
- Can kidney beans – 14.5 oz., drained
- Can chickpeas – 14.5 oz., drained
- Olive oil – 2 tbsps.
- Chili powder – ½ tsp.
- Sumac – 1 tbsp.
- Garlic cloves – 2, grated
- Fresh mint leaves – ¼ cup, chopped
- Fresh parsley – ½ cup, chopped
- Bell pepper – 1, chopped
- Onion – 1, chopped
- Tomato – 1, chopped
- Pepper & salt, to taste

Directions:

Add all ingredients into the mixing bowl and mix everything well. Serve.

Quinoa Apple Cranberry Salad

Cook time: 15 minutes | Serves: 6 | Per Serving: Calories 218, Carbs 33g, Fat 8g, Protein 5g

Ingredients:

For salad:

- Dried cranberries – 1/3 cup
- Toasted pecans – 1/3 cup, chopped
- Apple – 1 cup, diced
- Green onions – 2, sliced

- Celery – 1/2 cup, chopped
- Quinoa – 1 cup, uncooked

For dressing:

- Granulated garlic – ¼ tsp.
- Dijon mustard – 2 tsps.
- Olive oil – 1 tbsp.
- Honey – 1 tbsp.
- Apple cider vinegar – 2 tbsps.
- Pepper & salt, to taste

Directions:

Cook quinoa according to packet instructions and let it cool. In a small bowl, whisk together all dressing ingredients and set aside. In a mixing bowl, add quinoa and remaining salad ingredients and mix well. Pour dressing over salad and mix well. Serve.

Feta Avocado Chickpea Salad

Cook time: 5 minutes | Serves: 4 | Per Serving: Calories 194, Carbs 27.2g, Fat 6.4g, Protein 7.7g

Ingredients:

- Feta cheese – 1/3 cup, crumbled
- Lime juice – 1
- Green onion – 2 tbsps., chopped
- Fresh cilantro – 1/3 cup., chopped
- Avocados – 2, pitted and chopped
- Can chickpeas – 14 oz., drained and rinsed
- Pepper & salt, to taste

Directions:

Add all ingredients into the mixing bowl and mix everything well. Serve.

Tomato Avocado Salad

Cook time: 5 minutes | Serves: 3 | Per Serving: Calories 405, Carbs 13g, Fat 35g, Protein 14g

Ingredients:

- Olives – 5, halved and deseed
- Avocado – 1, peel and sliced
- Tomatoes – 4, sliced
- Olive oil – 2 tbsps.
- Pesto – 2 tbsps.
- Mozzarella cheese – 4 oz
- Pepper & salt, to taste

Directions:

Add avocado, olives, and tomato in a mixing bowl and mix well. Add olive oil, pesto, and mozzarella. Season with pepper and salt. Toss well and serve.

Greek Salad

Cook time: 5 minutes | Serves: 4 | Per Serving: Calories 320, Carbs 14g, Fat 27g, Protein 9g

Ingredients:

- Oregano – 1 tsp, dried
- Feta cheese – 7 oz, crumbled
- Capers – 4 tbsps.
- Olives – 16
- Small onion – 1, sliced
- Green bell pepper – 1, sliced
- Tomatoes – 4, sliced
- Olive oil – 4 tbsps.
- Cucumber – 1, peel and sliced
- Pepper & salt, to taste

Directions:

Add all ingredients into the mixing bowl and toss well. Serve.

Egg Avocado Salad

Cook time: 5 minutes | Serves: 2 | Per Serving: Calories 490, Carbs 13g, Fat 40g, Protein 17g

Ingredients:

- Avocado – 1, peel and sliced
- Garlic cloves – 2, minced
- Sour cream – 1/2 cup
- Arugula – 4 cups
- large eggs – 4, hard-boiled, peel and chopped
- Dijon mustard – 2 tsps.
- Pepper & salt, to taste

Directions:

In a small bowl, mix together Dijon mustard, garlic, sour cream, pepper, and salt. In a mixing bowl, add eggs, arugula, and avocado and toss well. Pour dressing over salad and mix well. Serve.

Lettuce Salad

Cook time: 5 minutes | Serves: 2 | Per Serving: Calories 136, Carbs 11g, Fat 10g, Protein 1.1g

Ingredients:

- Tomato – 1, chopped
- Romaine lettuce – 2 cups, chopped
- For dressing:
- Lemon juice – 2 tsps.
- Mayonnaise – 1/4 cup
- Liquid stevia – 3 drops
- Apple cider vinegar – 2 tsps.

Directions:

In a small bowl, whisk together all dressing ingredients and set aside. In a large bowl, add chopped romaine lettuce and tomato and mix well. Pour dressing over salad and toss well. Serve.

Dill Tomato Cucumber Salad

Cook time: 5 minutes | Serves: 4 | Per Serving: Calories 85, Carbs 7g, Fat 6g, Protein 2g

Ingredients:

- Large cucumber – 1, peeled & sliced
- Tomato – 1, sliced
- Sour cream – 1/2 cup
- Dill – 1 tsp.
- Lemon juice – 2 tsps.
- Small onion – 1, sliced
- Salt – 1/4 tsp.

Directions:

In a mixing bowl, add sour cream, lemon juice, dill, and salt and mix well. Add tomato, cucumber, and onion and stir well to coat. Serve.

Olive Cucumber Salad

Cook time: 5 minutes | Serves: 2 | Per Serving: Calories 66, Carbs 10g, Fat 2.8g, Protein 1.7g

Ingredients:

- Olives – 1/4 cup, sliced
- Cherry tomatoes – 1/2 cup, cut in half
- Cucumber – 1, chopped
- Olive oil vinaigrette – 1/4 cup
- Onion – 1/2, chopped
- Pepper & salt, to taste

Directions:

Add all ingredients into the mixing bowl and toss well. Place salad bowl in the fridge for hours. Serve.

Cucumber Jalapeno Salad

Cook time: 5 minutes | Serves: 4 | Per Serving: Calories 85, Carbs 7.3g, Fat 6.1g, Protein 2g

Ingredients:

- Sour cream – 1/2 cup
- Fresh cilantro – 2 tbsps., chopped
- Fresh lime juice – 2 tbsps.
- Tomatoes – 1/2 cup, diced
- Onion – 1/4 cup, chopped
- Cucumbers – 4 cups, peeled and diced
- Garlic clove – 1, crushed
- Jalapeno pepper – 2, seeded and diced
- Seasoning salt – 1 tbsp.

Directions:

Add all ingredients into the large mixing bowl and mix well. Place salad bowl in the fridge for 2 hours. Serve.

Creamy Dill Egg Salad

Cook time: 5 minutes | Serves: 4 | Per Serving: Calories 140, Carbs 4g, Fat 10g, Protein 8g

Ingredients:

- Fresh dill – 1 tbsp., chopped
- Mayonnaise – 3 tbsps.
- Dill pickles – 1/2 cup, chopped
- Hard-boiled eggs – 6, chopped
- Pepper – 1/4 tsp.
- Salt –1/4 tsp.

Directions:

Add all ingredients into the mixing bowl and mix well. Serve.

Mustard Egg Cauliflower Salad

Cook time: 5 minutes | Serves: 8 | Per Serving: Calories 110, Carbs 6g, Fat 7g, Protein 6g

Ingredients:

- Hard-boiled eggs – 6, peeled and chopped
- Mayonnaise – 1/3 cup
- Head cauliflower – 1, steamed and cut into florets
- Onion – 2 tbsps., chopped
- Mustard – 3 tbsps.

Directions:

Add all ingredients into the mixing bowl and mix well. Place bowl in the fridge for hours. Serve.

Greek Avocado Salad

Cook time: 5 minutes | Serves: 4 | Per Serving: Calories 304, Carbs 12g, Fat 25g, Protein 10g

Ingredients:

- Olives – 1/2 cup, pitted
- Feta cheese – 7 oz, cubed
- Onion – 1/2, sliced
- large cucumber – 1, sliced
- Avocado – 1, diced
- Bell pepper – 1, sliced
- Tomatoes – 4, chopped
- For dressing:
- Red wine vinegar – 2 tbsps.
- Olive oil – 1/4 cup
- Oregano – 2 tsps.
- Garlic – 1 tsp., minced
- Salt – 1/4 tsp.

Directions:

In a small bowl, mix together all dressing ingredients and set aside. Add all salad ingredients into the mixing bowl and mix well. Pour dressing over salad and toss well. Serve.

Basil Tomato Cucumber Salad

Cook time: 5 minutes | Serves: 6 | Per Serving: Calories 100, Carbs 5g, Fat 8g, Protein 1g

Ingredients:

- Cucumbers – 3 cups, sliced
- Onion – 1/3 cup, chopped
- Tomatoes – 3, sliced
- Basil – 1/4 cup, chopped
- For dressing:
- Dill weeds – 1/2 tsp.
- Red wine vinegar – 1/2 tbsp.
- Apple cider vinegar – 3/4 cup
- Olive oil – 1/4 cup
- Pepper – 1/4 tsp.
- Salt – 1/4 tsp.

Directions:

In a small bowl, mix together all dressing ingredients. In a large mixing bowl, add all salad ingredients and mix well. Pour dressing over salad and toss well. Serve.

Cabbage Carrot Salad

Cook time: 5 minutes | Serves: 4 | Per Serving: Calories 35, Carbs 8g, Fat 0.1g, Protein 1.3g

Ingredients:

- Cabbage – 3 cups, shredded
- Dill – 1/4 tsp.
- Green pepper – 1, chopped
- Carrot – 1, shredded
- Turnip – 1, shredded
- Salt – 1 tsp.

Directions:

Add cabbage and salt in a bowl. Cover bowl and set aside for 40 minutes. Wash cabbage and dry well. Add cabbage in a mixing bowl with remaining ingredients and toss well. Serve.

Nutritious Summer Salad

Cook time: 5 minutes | Serves: 6 | Per Serving: Calories 105, Carbs 5g, Fat 9g, Protein 1g

Ingredients:

- Red cabbage – 1 cup, chopped
- Yellow bell pepper – 1/3 cup, chopped
- Red bell pepper – 1/2 cup, chopped
- Scallions – 1/4 cup, chopped
- Cauliflower – 3 cups, chopped
- Fresh basil – 1/4 cup, chopped
- Celery – 1/2 cup, chopped
- For dressing:
- Apple cider vinegar – 2 tbsps.
- Lime juice – 2 tsps.
- Olive oil – 1/4 cup
- Swerve – 2 tbsps.
- Ginger – 1 1/2 tbsps., minced
- Kosher salt – 1/2 tsp.

Directions:

Add all vegetables in a large mixing bowl and toss well. In a small bowl, mix together all dressing ingredients and pour over salad. Toss well and Serve.

Caprese Salad

Cook time: 5 minutes | Serves: 5 | Per Serving: Calories 295, Carbs 8g, Fat 25g, Protein 10.2g

Ingredients:

For salad:

- Marinated artichoke hearts – 6.5 oz.
- Mozzarella cheese – 6 oz.
- Herb seasoning – 1 tsp.
- Cherry tomatoes – 6 oz.
- Black olives – 6 oz., pitted

For vinaigrette:

- Water – 1 tbsp.
- Vinegar – 2 tbsps.
- Olive oil – 1/4 cup
- Lemon zest – 1 tsp.
- Erythritol – 1 tsp.
- Salt – 1/8 tsp.

Directions:

Add all salad ingredients in a mixing bowl and mix well. In a small bowl, mix together all dressing ingredients and pour over salad. Toss salad well and place it in the fridge for 1 hour. Serve.

Classic Egg Salad

Cook time: 5 minutes │Serves: 1 │ Per Serving: Calories 235, Carbs 14g, Fat 13g, Protein 16g

Ingredients:

- Hard-boiled eggs – 2, peeled and sliced
- Red cabbage – 1/3 cup, shredded
- Carrots – 1/4 cup, shredded
- Spinach leaves – 1/2 cup
- Lettuce – 1 1/2 cups
- Peas – 4 tbsps.
- Sunflower seeds – 3 tbsps.

Directions:

Add all ingredients into the large bowl and mix well. Serve.

Strawberry Spinach Salad

Cook time: 5 minutes │Serves: 4 │ Per Serving: Calories 285, Carbs 12g, Fat 25g, Protein 4.5g

Ingredients:

- Avocado – 1, chopped
- Mozzarella balls – 1 cup, halved
- Strawberries – 1 cup, quartered
- Spinach – 4 cups

- Basil – 1/4 cup, chopped
- Cherry tomatoes – 1/2 cup, halved
- For dressing:
- Red wine vinegar – 2 tbsps.
- Mayonnaise – 3 tbsps.
- Olive oil – 3 tbsps.
- Dried oregano – 1/2 tsp.
- Garlic cloves – 2, minced
- Balsamic vinegar – 1 1/2 tbsps.
- Pepper & salt, to taste

Directions:

In a large bowl, toss together avocado, basil, mozzarella, strawberries, and tomatoes. Divide spinach between four serving plates and top with avocado mixture. In a small bowl, whisk together all dressing ingredients. Drizzle dressing over salad. Serve.

Broccoli Cauliflower Salad

Cook time: 5 minutes | Serves: 7 | Per Serving: Calories 250, Carbs 14g, Fat 19g, Protein 35g

Ingredients:

- Cauliflower florets – 8 oz.
- Broccoli florets – 8 oz.
- Red bell pepper – 2 oz., diced
- Green onion – 2 tbsps., chopped
- Cheddar cheese – 4 oz., cubed
- For dressing:
- Sour cream – 3/4 cup
- Mayonnaise – 3/4 cup
- Fresh lemon juice – 1 tbsp.
- Swerve – 2 tbsps.

Directions:

Add all salad ingredients into the large bowl and toss well. In a small bowl, whisk together all dressing ingredients and pour over salad. Toss well and place in the fridge for 2 hours. Serve.

Cabbage Cucumber Salad

Cook time: 5 minutes | Serves: 8 | Per Serving: Calories 70, Carbs 6g, Fat 5g, Protein 1.3g

Ingredients:

- Cucumbers – 2, sliced
- Fresh dill – 2 tbsps., chopped
- Cabbage head – 1/2., chopped
- Olive oil – 3 tbsps.

- Lemon juice – 1/2
- Green onion – 2 tbsps., chopped
- Pepper & salt, to taste

Directions:

Add cabbage into the large bowl. Season with 1 teaspoon of salt mix well and set aside. Add cucumbers, green onions, and dill. Mix well. Add lemon juice, pepper, olive oil, and salt. Mix well. Place salad bowl in the fridge for 2 hours. Serve.

Radish Cucumber Salad

Cook time: 5 minutes | Serves: 4 | Per Serving: Calories 115, Carbs 6.7g, Fat 9g, Protein 2g

Ingredients:

- Cucumber – 1, sliced
- Dill – 1/4 cup, chopped
- Radishes – 10, sliced
- Sour cream – 3/4 cup
- Chives – 2 tbsps., chopped
- Pepper & salt, to taste

Directions:

In a mixing bowl, mix cucumber, dill, chives, and radishes. In a small bowl, whisk together sour cream, pepper, and salt. Pour dressing over salad and toss well. Serve.

Soups & Stews

Lentil Kale Soup

Cook time: 40 minutes | Serves: 8 | Per Serving: Calories 215, Carbs 14g, Fat 17g, Protein 5g

Ingredients:

- Lentils – ½ cup
- Kale – 1 cup, chopped
- Celery stalk – 1, chopped
- Carrot – 1, peeled and chopped
- Onion – 1, chopped
- Water – 1 cup
- Coconut milk – 2 cups
- Bay leaf – 1
- Vegetable stock – 3 cups
- Olive oil – 1 tbsp.
- Pepper – ½ tsp.
- Salt – ½ tsp.

Directions:

Heat oil in a saucepan over medium heat. Add onion and sauté for 2 minutes. Add celery and carrot and cook for 5 minutes. Add lentils and stir well and cook for 2 minutes. Add bay leaf and stock. Bring to boil. Turn heat to low and simmer for 20 minutes. Add coconut milk and stir well and cook for 10 minutes more. Season with pepper and salt. Discard bay leaf from soup. Puree the soup using a blender until smooth. Serve.

Easy Split Pea Soup

Cook time: 8 hours | Serves: 6 | Per Serving: Calories 319, Carbs 51.9g, Fat 2.3g, Protein 24.1g

Ingredients:

- Dried green split peas – 16 oz
- Bay leaf – 1
- Vegetable broth – 6 cups
- Fresh parsley – ¼ cup, chopped
- Garlic clove – 1, minced
- Large carrots – 2, diced
- Celery stalks – 3, diced
- Leek – 1, chopped
- Pepper – ½ tsp.
- Salt – 1 tsp.

Directions:

Add all ingredients into the slow cooker and stir well. Cover slow cooker with lid and cook on low for 8 hours. Discard bay leaf. Stir and serve.

Pasta Swiss Chard Soup

Cook time: 25 minutes | Serves: 10 Per Serving: Calories 65, Carbs 8g, Fat 3g, Protein 1.6g

Ingredients:

- Swiss chard – 8 oz., shredded
- Leek – 1, chopped
- Onion – 1/2, diced
- Lemon juice – 2 tbsps.
- Whole wheat pasta – 1 cup, cooked
- Vegetable stock – 6 cups.
- Dried thyme – ¼ tsp.
- Garlic cloves – 2, minced
- Olive oil – 2 tbsps.
- Pepper – ¼ tsp.
- Salt – ½ tsp.

Directions:

Heat oil in a saucepan over medium heat. Add leek and onion and sauté for 5 minutes. Add Swiss chard, garlic, thyme, pepper, and salt and cook for 5 minutes. Add stock and stir well. Bring to boil. Turn heat to low and simmer for 10 minutes. Transfer 1 cup chard mixture to the blender and blend until smooth. Return blended soup to the saucepan along with lemon juice and pasta. Stir well. Serve.

Coconut Broccoli Soup

Cook time: 25 minutes | Serves: 4 | Per Serving: Calories 245, Carbs 28g, Fat 15g, Protein 4g

Ingredients:

- Broccoli florets – 2 cups
- Vegetable stock – 4 cups
- Olive oil – 1 tbsp.
- Butternut squash – 4 cups, diced
- Coconut milk – 1 cup
- Chili paste – 1 tsp.
- Ginger – 1 tbsp., minced
- Garlic cloves – 3, minced
- Onion – 1, chopped
- Bay leaf – 1

Directions:

Heat oil in a pot over medium heat. Add onion and bay leaf and sauté for 5 minutes. Add chili paste, ginger, and garlic and sauté for a minute. Add broccoli, squash, and stock and stir well. Bring to boil. Turn heat to medium-low and simmer for 20 minutes. Discard bay leaf from soup. Remove pot from heat and puree the soup using a blender until smooth. Stir in coconut milk. Serve.

Delicious Chickpea Stew

Cook time: 6 hours 10 minutes | Serves: 5 | Per Serving: Calories 295, Carbs 51g, Fat 6g, Protein 10.7g

Ingredients:

- Can chickpeas – 30 oz, rinsed and drained
- Fresh parsley – ¼ cup
- Fresh spinach – 2 cups
- Tomatoes – 2 ½ cups, chopped
- Balsamic vinegar – 2 tsps.
- Ground coriander – 2 tsps.
- Fresh ginger – 2 tbsps., minced
- Garlic – 1 tbsp., chopped
- Onions – 2, chopped
- Olive oil – 1 ½ tbsps.
- Pepper – ½ tsp.
- Salt – 1 tsp.

Directions:

Heat olive oil in a large pan over medium heat. Add onion and sauté for 10 minutes or until onion is lightly brown. Add garlic, ground coriander, ginger, pepper, and salt and stir for a minute. Stir in tomatoes and balsamic vinegar. Add chickpeas into the slow cooker then pour tomato mixture over the chickpeas and stir well. Cover slow cooker with lid and cook on low for 6 hours. Add parsley and spinach just before serving and stir. Serve.

Healthy Smooth Broccoli Soup

Cook time: 20 minutes | Serves: 6 | Per Serving: Calories 65, Carbs 12g, Fat 0.5g, Protein 3.4g

Ingredients:

- Broccoli florets – 5 cups, chopped
- Olive oil – 1 tbsp.
- Bell pepper – 1 cup, chopped
- Onion – 1, chopped
- Garlic cloves – 3, minced
- Half and half – ¼ cup
- Vegetable stock – 32 oz.
- Celery –1 cup, chopped

Directions:

Heat oil in a saucepan over medium-high heat. Add onion, garlic, celery, and bell pepper and sauté until tender. Stir in stock and broccoli. Bring to boil. Turn heat to low and simmer until broccoli softens. Remove saucepan from heat and let sit for 10 minutes. Puree the soup using a blender until smooth. Add half and half and stir well. Serve.

Simple Tomato Soup

Cook time: 35 minutes │Serves: 2 │ Per Serving: Calories 328, Carbs 23.5g, Fat 24.1g, Protein 7.8g

Ingredients:

- Can tomatoes – 28 oz.
- Vegetable broth – 1 ½ cups
- Onion – ½, chopped
- Butter – 4 tbsps.
- Salt – ½ tsp.

Directions:

Melt butter in a medium saucepan over medium heat. Add onion and sauté for 2-3 minutes. Add broth, tomatoes, and salt stir well. Simmer for 25-30 minutes. Puree the soup using a blender until smooth. Serve.

Barley Vegetable Soup

Cook time: 8 hours │Serves: 10 │ Per Serving: Calories 114, Carbs 20.9g, Fat 1.1g, Protein 5.7g

Ingredients:

- Pearl barley – ¾ cup
- Fresh parsley – ¼ cup, minced
- Water – 2 cups
- Vegetable broth – 6 cups
- Can tomatoes – 14 oz, diced
- Dried thyme – ¾ tsp.
- Dried oregano – 1 tsp.
- Paprika – 1 tsp.
- Frozen green beans– 1 ½ cups
- Garlic– 1 tbsp.
- Sweet potato – 1, peeled and cut into ¾-inch pieces
- Celery stalks – 2, chopped
- Carrots – 2, chopped
- Onion– 1, chopped
- Pepper– ½ tsp.
- Salt – ½ tsp.

Directions:

Add all ingredients except parsley into the slow cooker and stir well. Cover slow cooker with lid and cook on low for 8 hours or until barley is tender. Stir in parsley. Serve.

Flavorful Tomato Soup

Cook time: 35 minutes | Serves: 8 | Per Serving: Calories 175, Carbs 10g, Fat 12g, Protein 4.5g

Ingredients:

- Can whole tomatoes – 28 oz., peeled
- Flour – 2 tbsps.
- Garlic cloves – 2, minced
- Onion – 1, chopped
- Butter – 2 tbsps.
- Heavy cream – 1 cup
- Sugar – 1 tsp.
- Tomato paste – 3 oz.
- Vegetable broth – 4 cups
- Olive oil – 2 tbsps.
- Pepper & salt, to taste

Directions:

Heat oil and butter in a pan over medium heat. Add garlic and onion and sauté for 2-3 minutes. Add flour, pepper, and salt and stir for 30 seconds. Slowly add broth while whisking. Add tomato paste, tomatoes, and sugar and stir well. Turn heat to low and simmer for 20 minutes. Puree the soup using a blender until smooth. Add cream and stir well and cook for 5 minutes more. Serve.

Healthy Lentil Soup

Cook time: 30 minutes | Serves: 6 | Per Serving: Calories 305, Carbs 36g, Fat 12g, Protein 14g

Ingredients:

- Can tomatoes – 15 oz., crushed
- Red lentils – 1 ½ cups
- Curry powder – 1 tbsp.
- Ginger – 1 tbsp., minced
- Can coconut milk – 7 oz.
- Water – 6 cups.
- Garlic – 1 tbsp., minced
- Onion – 1, diced
- Olive oil – 2 tbsps.
- Salt – 1 ½ tsp.

Directions:

Heat oil in a large pot over medium heat. Add garlic, onion, and ginger and sauté until onion is softened. Add curry powder and stir for 2 minutes. Add lentils and stir and cook for 2 minutes.

Add tomatoes, water, and salt and stir well. Bring to simmer for 20 minutes. Add coconut milk and stir well. Turn heat to low and cook for 10 minutes more. Serve.

Creamy Pumpkin Soup

Cook time: 15 minutes | Serves: 1 | Per Serving: Calories 430, Carbs 15g, Fat 42g, Protein 3g

Ingredients:

- Pumpkin puree – ½ cup
- Curry powder – ¼ tsp.
- Garlic clove – 1, chopped
- Onion – 1 tbsp., chopped
- Water – 1/3 cup
- Vegetable bouillon – 1 tsp
- Coconut milk – ¼ cup
- Olive oil – 2 tsps.
- Pepper & salt, to taste

Directions:

Heat oil in a pan over medium heat. Add garlic, onion, curry powder, pepper, and salt and sauté until onion is softened about 3-5 minutes. Add remaining ingredients and stir well and simmer until heated through. Puree the soup using a blender until smooth. Serve.

Lentil Carrot Tomato Soup

Cook time: 30 minutes | Serves: 6 | Per Serving: Calories 195, Carbs 33g, Fat 4.8g, Protein 10g

Ingredients:

- Red lentils – 1 cup
- Can tomatoes – 28 oz., diced
- Vegetable stock – 6 cups
- Carrots – 3, diced
- Onion – 1, diced
- Garlic cloves – 4, minced
- Lemon juice – 1 tbsp.
- Bay leaves – 2
- Ground thyme – ½ tsp.
- Dried basil – 1 tsp.
- Dried oregano – 1 tsp.
- Olive oil – 1 tbsp.
- Pepper & salt, to taste

Directions:

Heat oil in a large pot over medium heat. Add carrots, onion, and garlic and sauté for 5 minutes. Add tomatoes, lentils, stock, herbs, and spices and bring to boil. Turn heat to low and simmer until lentils are softened, for about 20-25 minutes. Season with pepper and salt. Stir in lemon juice. Discard bay leaves. Stir well. Serve.

Creamy Parmesan Tomato Soup

Cook time: 20 minutes | Serves: 8 | Per Serving: Calories 165, Carbs 5.6g, Fat 10.9g, Protein 9.6g

Ingredients:

- Can whole tomatoes – 28 oz., peeled
- Parmesan cheese – 1 cup, grated
- Heavy cream – 1 cup
- Garlic – 2 tbsps., minced
- Vegetable broth – 4 cups
- Pepper & salt, to taste

Directions:

Puree tomatoes in a blender. Pour tomatoes, garlic, and broth into the large pot and bring to boil over medium heat. Turn heat to low and simmer for 2-3 minutes. Remove pot from heat. Add parmesan cheese and cream and stir well and simmer over low heat for 15 minutes. Puree the soup using a blender until smooth. Season with pepper and salt. Serve.

Carrot Soup

Cook time: 45 minutes | Serves: 6 | Per Serving: Calories 130, Carbs 21g, Fat 6g, Protein 2g

Ingredients:

- Carrots – 2 lbs., peeled and sliced
- Vegetable stock – 4 cups
- Garlic cloves – 5, smashed
- Leeks – 2, sliced
- Olive oil – 2 tbsps.
- Ground cumin – ½ tsp.
- Ground coriander – ¼ tsp.
- Pepper & salt, to taste

Directions:

Heat olive oil in a saucepan over medium heat. Add carrots, cumin, coriander, garlic, leek, pepper, and salt and cook for 15 minutes. Add stock and stir well. Bring to boil. Turn heat to low and simmer for 30 minutes. Puree the soup using a blender until smooth. Serve.

Tomato Green Bean Soup

Cook time: 35 minutes | Serves: 8 | Per Serving: Calories 65, Carbs 11g, Fat 3.5g, Protein 2g

Ingredients:

- Green beans – 1 lb., cut into 1-inch pieces
- Tomatoes – 3 cups, chopped
- Fresh basil – ¼ cup, chopped
- Carrots – 1 cup, chopped
- Onion – 1 cup, chopped
- Garlic cloves – 2, minced
- Vegetable stock – 6 cups
- Olive oil – 1 tbsp.
- Pepper – ¼ tsp.
- Salt – ½ tsp.

Directions:

Heat oil in a saucepan over medium heat. Add carrots and onion to the pan and sauté for 5 minutes. Add garlic, beans, and stock and stir well. Bring to boil. Turn heat low and simmer for 20 minutes. Add basil, tomatoes, pepper, and salt. Stir well. Cover and simmer for 5 minutes more. Serve.

Creamy Mushroom Soup

Cook time: 25 minutes | Serves: 4 | Per Serving: Calories 60, Carbs 8g, Fat 1.4g, Protein 4.1g

Ingredients:

- Mushrooms – 3 cups, sliced
- Onion – 1, chopped
- Olive oil – 1 tsp.
- Milk – 1 cup
- Whole wheat flour – 2 tsp.
- Pepper & salt, to taste

Directions:

Heat oil in a saucepan over medium heat. Add onion sauté over medium heat for 1 minute. Add mushrooms, flour, and 1 cup of water and stir well and cook for 5 minutes. Remove pan from heat and set aside to cool. Once it cools completely then add milk and blend using a blender until smooth. Season with pepper and salt. Add one cup of water and stir well and cook over medium heat for 2-3 minutes more. Serve.

Nutritious Spinach Soup

Cook time: 20 minutes | Serves: 4 | Per Serving: Calories 200, Carbs 18g, Fat 15g, Protein 5g

Ingredients:

- Spinach – 1 lb., stems trimmed
- Green onions – ½ cup, chopped
- Onion – 1, chopped
- Olive oil – 2 tbsps.
- Vegetable stock – 4 cups

- Potato – 1, peeled and chopped
- Garlic cloves – 3, minced
- Heavy cream – ½ cup
- Pepper & salt, to taste

Directions:

Heat oil in a pot over medium heat. Add green onions and onion and sauté until softened, about 5 minutes. Add spinach, potato, and garlic. Stir well. Pour stock and bring to boil. Stir well and cook for 15 minutes. Season with pepper and salt. Puree the soup using a blender until smooth. Serve.

Zucchini Cauliflower Soup

Cook time: 25 minutes | Serves: 6 | Per Serving: Calories 75, Carbs 15g, Fat 1.3g, Protein 5.3g

Ingredients:

- Large cauliflower head – 1, chopped
- Milk – 1 cup
- Vegetable stock – 3 cups
- Zucchinis – 2, peeled and chopped
- Olive oil – 1 tbsp.
- Basil – ½ tsp.
- Garlic – 1 tbsp., minced
- Large onion – 1., minced
- Pepper – ¼ tsp.
- Salt – ¼ tsp.

Directions:

Heat oil in a large saucepan over medium heat. Add onion and garlic and sauté for 5-10 minutes. Add zucchini, cauliflower, seasonings, and stock and stir well. Bring to boil. Turn heat to low and simmer for 15 minutes. Slowly add milk and stir well. Serve.

Carrot Cauliflower Soup

Cook time: 48 minutes | Serves: 8 | Per Serving: Calories 55, Carbs 10.5g, Fat 1.2g, Protein 1.8g

Ingredients:

- Cauliflower florets – 1 lb.
- Carrots – 1 lb., peeled and chopped
- Garlic cloves – 2, chopped
- Olive oil – ½ tbsp.
- Onion – 1, chopped
- Water – 2 ½ cups
- Vegetable stock – 2 ½ cups
- Ginger – 1 tsp., grated
- Pepper & salt, to taste

Directions:

Heat oil in a saucepan over medium heat. Add onion and sauté for 2-3 minutes. Add ginger, cauliflower, and carrots, and sauté for 5 minutes. Add water and stock and stir well. Bring to boil. Turn heat to low and simmer for 40 minutes. Remove saucepan from heat and let sit for 10 minutes. Puree the soup using a blender until smooth. Season with pepper and salt. Serve.

Coconut Carrot Tomato Soup

Cook time: 4 hours | Serves: 4 | Per Serving: Calories 190, Carbs 16g, Fat 14g, Protein 3g

Ingredients:

- Medium carrots – 4, peeled and chopped
- Turmeric – 1 tbsp.
- Coconut milk – 1 cup
- Can tomatoes – 14.5 oz, diced
- Ground cumin – 1 tsp.
- Ground coriander – 1 tsp.

Directions:

Add all ingredients into the slow cooker and stir well. Cover and cook on low for 4 hours. Puree the soup using a blender until smooth. Serve.

Basil Tomato Soup

Cook time: 30 minutes | Serves: 4 | Per Serving: Calories 136, Carbs 20g, Fat 5g, Protein 4g

Ingredients:

- Tomato – 14 oz, diced
- Tomato puree – 21 oz.
- Fennel bulbs – 2 ½ cups, chopped
- Butter – 1 ½ tbsps.
- Coriander – 2 tsps.
- Fresh basil – ½ cup, chopped
- Vegetable broth – ½ cup
- Pepper & salt, to taste

Directions:

Melt butter in a saucepan over medium heat. Add fennel and sauté for 10 minutes over medium-high heat. Add tomatoes, coriander, broth, and tomato puree and stir well. Bring to boil. Turn heat to low and simmer for 20 minutes. Remove from heat and stir in basil. Season soup with pepper and salt. Serve.

Coconut Spinach Soup

Cook time: 7 minutes | Serves: 4 | Per Serving: Calories 155, Carbs 4.2g, Fat 15g, Protein 2g

Ingredients:

- Baby spinach – 3 cups, wash, drained, and chopped
- Olive oil – 1 tsp.
- Coconut milk – 1 cup
- Water – 1 1/2 cups
- Pepper & salt, to taste

Directions:

Heat oil in a saucepan over medium heat. Add spinach and sauté for 2 minutes. Add 1 1/2 cups of water and stir well. Bring to boil for 2-3 minutes. Remove saucepan from heat and allow to cool slightly. Blend spinach mixture using a blender until smooth. Transfer blended spinach mixture into the saucepan. Add coconut milk, pepper, and salt. Stir well and cook for 2 minutes. Serve.

Easy Onion Soup

Cook time: 20 minutes | Serves: 6 | Per Serving: Calories 105, Carbs 15g, Fat 4g, Protein 1.7g

Ingredients:

- Onions – 8 cups, peel and slice
- Balsamic vinegar – 1 tbsp.
- Olive oil – 2 tbsps.
- Bay leaf – 1
- Vegetable stock – 6 cups
- Salt – 1 tsp.

Directions:

Add oil in the instant pot and set the pot on sauté mode. Add onion and cook until softened. Add remaining ingredients and stir well. Seal pot with lid and cook on high pressure for 10 minutes. Once done, allow release pressure naturally. Open the lid. Discard bay leaves. Puree the soup using a blender until smooth. Serve.

Lentil Spinach Soup

Cook time: 25 minutes | Serves: 4 | Per Serving: Calories 265, Carbs 37g, Fat 4.7g, Protein 19g

Ingredients:

- Fresh spinach – 6 cups
- Ground cumin – 2 tsp.
- Garlic cloves – 2, minced
- Celery stalk – 1, diced
- Turmeric – 1 tsp.
- Onion – 1/2, diced
- Olive oil – 2 tsps.
- Carrots – 2, peeled and diced

- Vegetable stock – 4 cups
- Brown lentils – 1 cup, rinsed
- Thyme – 1 tsp., dried
- Pepper – 1/4 tsp.
- Salt – 1/2 tsp.

Directions:

Add oil into the instant pot and set the pot on sauté mode. Add celery, onion, and carrots and sauté for 5 minutes. Add thyme, turmeric, cumin, garlic, pepper, and salt and stir for minute. Add broth and lentils and stir well. Seal pot with lid and cook on high pressure for 12 minutes. Release pressure using the quick-release method. Open the lid. Stir in spinach. Serve.

Zucchini Soup

Cook time: 28 minutes | Serves: 4 | Per Serving: Calories 200, Carbs 10.8g, Fat 18g, Protein 2.8g

Ingredients:

- Zucchini – 1, chopped
- Coconut milk – 1 cup
- Water – 1 cup
- Olive oil – 1 tbsp.
- Bell pepper – 1, chopped
- Carrots – 2, chopped

Directions:

Heat oil in a pan over medium heat. Add vegetables and cook for 7-8 minutes. Add coconut milk and stir well. Cook over medium heat for 5 minutes. Add water and cook on low for 15 minutes. Puree the soup using a blender until smooth. Season with pepper and salt. Serve.

Main Meals

Flavorful Lentil Sweet Potato Chili

Cook time: 8 hours | Serves: 6 | Per Serving: Calories 370, Carbs 54g, Fat 12g, Protein 14g

Ingredients:

- Sweet potatoes – 2, peeled and chopped
- Fresh spinach – 2 cups, chopped
- Vegetable broth – 4 cups
- Can tomatoes – 25 oz, crushed
- Paprika – 1 tsp.
- Cumin – 1 tsp.
- Chili powder – 1 tbsp.
- Corn – ½ cup
- Brown lentils – 1 cup
- Bell pepper – 2, chopped
- Garlic cloves – 2, minced
- Celery stalks – 3, chopped
- Onions – 2, diced
- Olive oil – 1 tbsp.
- Pepper – ½ tsp.
- Salt – 1 tsp.

Directions:

Add all ingredients except spinach into the slow cooker and stir everything well. Cover slow cooker with lid and cook on low for 8 hours or until lentil and sweet potatoes are tender. Stir in spinach. Serve.

Sautéed Green Beans & Carrots

Cook time: 10 minutes | Serves: 2 | Per Serving: Calories 230, Carbs 16g, Fat 18g, Protein 2g

Ingredients:

- Green beans – 2 cups, trimmed
- Fresh lemon juice – 1 tbsp.
- Butter – 2 tbsps.
- Baby carrots – 1 cup, halved lengthwise
- Olive oil – 1 tbsp.
- Pepper & salt, to taste

Directions:

Heat oil in a large pan over medium-high heat. Add carrots and cook for a minute. Add green beans and cook until beans are tender. Season with pepper and salt. Transfer vegetables on a plate. Turn heat to medium-low and add butter in the same pan. Once butter is melted then add lemon juice and stir well. Return vegetables to the pan and stir well to coat. Serve.

Sautéed Potato Zucchini

Cook time: 13 minutes | Serves: 1 | Per Serving: Calories 325, Carbs 18g, Fat 28g, Protein 3g

Ingredients:

- Zucchini – ½, cut into cubes
- Potato – ½, cut into cubes
- Fresh parsley – 1 tbsp., chopped
- Fresh chives – 1 tbsp., chopped
- Chili – 1, chopped
- Olive oil – 2 tbsps.
- Pepper & salt, to taste

Directions:

Heat oil in a pan over medium heat. Add potato to the pan and sauté for 4-5 minutes. Add zucchini and sauté for 4-5 minutes. Season with pepper and salt and cook for 2-3 minutes more. Add remaining ingredients and stir well. Serve.

Cranberry Brussels sprouts

Cook time: 10 minutes | Serves: 6 | Per Serving: Calories 170, Carbs 8g, Fat 13g, Protein 5g

Ingredients:

- Brussels sprouts – 1 lb., cut in half
- Blue cheese – ½ cup, crumbled
- Dried cranberries – ½ cup
- Pecans – ½ cup, toasted
- Vinegar – 1 tbsp.
- Olive oil – 3 tbsps.
- Pepper & salt, to taste

Directions:

Heat oil in a pan over medium-high heat. Add Brussels sprouts and cook for 5 minutes. Season with pepper and salt and cook for 5 minutes more. Drizzle with vinegar and stir well. Remove pan from heat. Transfer Brussels sprouts to a large mixing bowl and toss with cheese, pecans, and cranberries. Serve.

Easy Vegetarian Burritos

Cook time: 2 hours | Serves: 4 | Per Serving: Calories 350, Carbs 68g, Fat 4g, Protein 11g

Ingredients:

- Can black beans – 1 cup, drained & rinsed
- Taco seasoning – ¾ tsp.
- Can salsa – 1 cup
- Long grain rice – ¾ cup, rinsed
- Water – 1 ½ cups
- Can sweet corn – 1 cup, drained
- Large flour tortillas – 4
- Salt – ¼ tsp.

Directions:

Add beans, taco seasoning, salsa, rice, water, corn, and salt into the slow cooker and stir well. Cover slow cooker with lid and cook on low for 2 hours. Serve in flour tortillas with your favorite toppings.

Healthy Carrot Noodles

Cook time: 10 minutes | Serves: 4 | Per Serving: Calories 180, Carbs 5g, Fat 16g, Protein 5g

Ingredients:

- Carrots – 5, peeled and spiralized
- Vinegar – 1/4 cup
- Garlic – 1 tbsp., chopped
- Green onions – 1/4 cup, chopped
- Red chili flakes – 1 tsp.
- Olive oil – 1/4 cup
- Basil leaves – 1/2 cup
- Fresh parsley – 1 cup
- Pepper & salt, to taste

Directions:

Add red chili flakes, oil, vinegar, garlic, green onions, basil, and parsley into the blender and blend until smooth. Pour the blended paste into a large bowl. Add water in a saucepan with a pinch of salt and bring to boil. Add carrot noodles in boiling water and cook for 2 minutes. Add cooked noodles in a large bowl and toss with paste. Serve.

Mushroom Frittata

Cook time: 46 minutes | Serves: 4 | Per Serving: Calories 117, Carbs 5g, Fat 6g, Protein 10g

Ingredients:

- Eggs – 6
- Mushrooms – 6 oz., sliced
- Leeks – 1 cup, sliced
- Salt

Directions:

Preheat the oven to 350 F. Spray baking dish with cooking spray and set aside. Heat pan over medium heat. Spray pan with cooking spray. Add mushrooms, leeks, and salt in a pan sauté for 6 minutes. Break eggs in a bowl and whisk well. Transfer sautéed mushroom and leek mixture into the prepared dish. Pour egg mixture over mushroom mixture. Bake in a preheated oven for 40 minutes. Serve.

Asparagus Quiche

Cook time: 45 minutes | Serves: 6 | Per Serving: Calories 101, Carbs 4g, Fat 5g, Protein 11g

Ingredients:

- Eggs – 4
- Egg whites – 4
- Feta cheese – 2 tbsps., crumbled
- Cottage cheese – 1 cup
- Dried thyme – 1/2 tsp.
- Water – 1/4 cup
- Asparagus – 8 oz., cut into 1-inch pieces
- Black pepper – 1/4 tsp.
- Salt – 1/4 tsp.

Directions:

Preheat the oven to 375 F. Spray baking dish with cooking spray and set aside. Add water into the large pot and bring to boil over high heat. Add asparagus into the boiling water and cook for 2 minutes. Drain and rinse with cold water. In a large mixing bowl, whisk together egg whites, eggs, cottage cheese, thyme, water, pepper, and salt. Pour egg mixture into the prepared baking dish. Sprinkle asparagus pieces into the egg mixture then top with crumbled feta cheese. Bake for 30 minutes. Slice & serve.

Spinach Egg Bake

Cook time: 35 minutes | Serves: 6 | Per Serving: Calories 119, Carbs 2g, Fat 8g, Protein 10g

Ingredients:

- Eggs – 8, beaten
- Spike seasoning – 1 tsp.
- Green onion – 1/3 cup, sliced
- Mozzarella – 1 1/2 cups
- Olive oil – 1 tsp.
- Fresh spinach – 5 oz.
- Pepper & salt, to taste

Directions:

Preheat the oven to 375 F. Grease casserole dish and set aside. Heat oil in a large pan over medium heat. Add spinach and cook until wilted. Transfer cooked spinach into the casserole dish and spread well. Spread onion and cheese onto the spinach layer. In a small bowl, whisk together eggs, pepper, spike seasoning, and salt. Pour egg mixture over spinach mixture and stir gently. Bake for 35 minutes. Slice & serve.

Vegetarian Quinoa Chili

Cook time: 8 hours │Serves: 6 │ Per Serving: Calories 249, Carbs 45g, Fat 3g, Protein 11g

Ingredients:

- Quinoa – 1/3 cup
- Vegetable broth – 3 cups.
- Chili flakes – ½ tsp.
- Ground coriander – 1 tsp.
- Paprika – 1 tbsp.
- Cumin – 1 tbsp.
- Chili powder – 1 tbsp.
- Can chili beans – 30 oz.
- Can tomato sauce– 8 oz.
- Can fire-roasted tomatoes – 28 oz.
- Garlic cloves – 2, minced
- Red bell pepper – 1, chopped
- Poblano pepper – 1, diced
- Large onion– 1, chopped
- Salt– 1 tsp.

Directions:

Add all ingredients into the slow cooker and stir well. Cover slow cooker and cook on high for 2 hours. After 2 hours cook on low for 6 hours. Stir well and serve.

Stuffed Bell Pepper

Cook time: 25 minutes │Serves: 2 │ Per Serving: Calories 284, Carbs 5g, Fat 25g, Protein 11g

Ingredients:

- Medium bell peppers – 2, cut in half and deseeded
- Olive oil – 2 tbsps.
- Broccoli florets – 1/4 cup
- Cherry tomatoes – 1/4 cup
- Dried sage – 1 tsp.
- Cheddar cheese – 2.5 oz., grated
- Eggs – 4
- Almond milk – 7 oz.
- Pepper & salt, to taste

Directions:

Preheat the oven to 390 F. In a bowl, whisk together eggs, milk, broccoli, cherry tomatoes, sage, pepper, and salt. Add oil to the baking dish and spread well. Place bell pepper halves in the baking dish. Pour egg mixture into the bell pepper halves. Sprinkle cheese on top of bell pepper. Bake for 25 minutes. Serve.

Zucchini Eggplant with Cheese

Cook time: 40 minutes | Serves: 6 | Per Serving: Calories 110, Carbs 10g, Fat 5g, Protein 7g

Ingredients:

- Medium eggplant – 1, sliced
- Olive oil – 1 tbsp.
- Cherry tomatoes – 1 cup, halved
- Garlic cloves – 4, minced
- Parsley – 4 tbsps., chopped
- Basil – 4 tbsps., chopped
- Medium zucchini – 3, sliced
- Parmesan cheese – 3 oz., grated
- Pepper – 1/4 tsp.
- Salt – 1/4 tsp.

Directions:

Preheat the oven to 350 F. Spray baking dish with cooking spray. In a large bowl, add chopped cherry tomatoes, eggplant, zucchini, olive oil, garlic, cheese, basil, pepper, and salt toss well. Transfer the eggplant mixture into the baking dish and place dish in the oven. Bake for 35 minutes. Garnish with parsley and serve.

Veggie Egg Scramble

Cook time: 10 minutes | Serves: 1 | Per Serving: Calories 320, Carbs 4g, Fat 26g, Protein 17g

Ingredients:

- Eggs – 3, beaten
- Spinach – 1/2 cup, chopped
- Bell peppers – 1/4 cup, chopped
- Bella mushrooms – 4, sliced
- Coconut oil – 1 tbsp.
- Pepper & salt, to taste

Directions:

Melt 1/2 tbsp of oil in a pan over medium heat. Add vegetables and sauté for 5 minutes. Heat remaining oil in another pan and add beaten eggs into the pan and cook over medium heat, stirring constantly. Season eggs with pepper and salt. Add sautéed vegetables to egg mixture and mix well. Serve.

Zucchini Quiche

Cook time: 40 minutes | Serves: 6 | Per Serving: Calories 180, Carbs 8g, Fat 11g, Protein 13g

Ingredients:

- Eggs – 3
- Dried oregano – 1/2 tsp.
- Dried basil – 1/2 tsp.
- Olive oil – 1 tbsp.
- Mozzarella – 1 cup, shredded
- Ricotta – 15 oz.
- Onion – 1, chopped
- Medium zucchini – 2, sliced
- Pepper & salt, to taste

Directions:

Preheat the oven to 350 F. Sauté zucchini over low heat. Add onion and cook for 10 minutes. Add pepper and seasoning to the zucchini mixture. Beat eggs, and then add in mozzarella and ricotta. Fold in onions and zucchini. Spray pie dish with cooking spray. Pour egg mixture into the pie dish and bake for 30 minutes. Serve.

Pumpkin Chickpea Curry

Cook time: 4 hours | Serves: 6 | Per Serving: Calories 375, Carbs 70g, Fat 7g, Protein 12g

Ingredients:

- Pumpkin – 2 cups, peeled and diced
- Peanuts – 3 tbsps., crushed
- Spinach – 1 cup
- Can chickpeas – 15 oz, drained and rinsed
- Sweet potato – 2, peeled and cut into cubes
- Coconut sugar – 1 tbsp.
- Soy sauce – 1 ½ tbsps.
- Curry paste – 1 tbsp.
- Coconut milk – 1 cup
- Vegetable broth – 1 cup
- Garlic – 1 tbsp., minced
- Onion – 1, chopped
- Olive oil – ½ tbsp.

Directions:

Heat olive oil in a pan over medium-high heat. Add onion and sauté for 2-3 minutes. Turn heat to medium. Add garlic and sauté for 2 minutes more. Remove pan from heat. Add broth, coconut sugar, soy sauce, curry paste, and coconut milk to the slow cooker and stir to combine. Add sautéed onion and garlic along with chickpeas, sweet potato, and pumpkin and stir everything well. Cover slow cooker with lid and cook on high for 4 hours. 10 minutes before serving add spinach and stir well. Serve over rice.

Spinach Broccoli Coconut Curry

Cook time: 30 minutes | Serves: 4 | Per Serving: Calories 225, Carbs 6g, Fat 23g, Protein 2g

Ingredients:

- Coconut cream – 1/2 cup
- Onion – 1/4, sliced
- Coconut oil – 4 tbsps.
- Spinach – 1/2 cup
- Broccoli florets – 1 cup
- Curry paste – 1 tbsp.
- Soy sauce – 2 tsps.
- Ginger – 1 tsp., minced
- Garlic – 1 tsp., minced

Directions:

Heat 2 tbsps. coconut oil in a pan over a medium-high heat. Add onion and cook until softened. Add garlic and sauté for 2 minutes. Turn heat to medium-low and add broccoli and stir well. Once broccoli is cooked then move vegetables to the other side of the pan. Add curry paste and cook for a minute. Add spinach and cook until wilted. Add coconut cream, remaining oil, ginger, and soy sauce. Stir well and simmer for 5 minutes. Serve.

Cauliflower Mac and Cheese

Cook time: 20 minutes | Serves: 4 | Per Serving: Calories 430, Carbs 13g, Fat 35g, Protein 20g

Ingredients:

- Heavy cream – 1 cup
- Garlic powder – 1/8 tsp.
- Pepper – 1/4 tsp.
- Cheddar cheese – 2 cups, shredded
- Dijon mustard – 1 tsp.
- Cream cheese – 2 oz.
- Large cauliflower head – 1, cut into florets
- Kosher salt – 1/2 tsp.

Directions:

Preheat the oven to 375 F. Add water and salt to the pot and bring to boil. Spray a baking dish with cooking spray and set aside. Add cauliflower florets into the boiling water and cook for 5 minutes. Drain well and transfer to a baking dish. Add cream into the saucepan and bring to simmer, whisk in mustard and cream cheese until smooth. Stir in 1 1/2 cups of cheese, plus pepper, garlic, and salt. Whisk until cheese melts for 2 minutes.. Remove pan from heat and pour over cauliflower florets and stir well. Top with remaining cheese and bake for 15 minutes. Serve.

Baked Herb Zucchini

Cook time: 35 minutes | Serves: 6 | Per Serving: Calories 105, Carbs 10g, Fat 4g, Protein 8g

Ingredients:

- Zucchini – 2 1/2 lbs., cut into quarters
- Parsley – 1/3 cup, chopped
- Dried basil – 1 tsp.
- Parmesan cheese – 1/2 cup, shredded
- Garlic cloves – 6, crushed
- Cherry tomatoes – 10 oz., cut in half
- Pepper – 1/2 tsp.
- Salt – 3/4 tsp.

Directions:

Preheat the oven to 350 F. Spray baking dish with cooking spray and set aside. Add all ingredients except parsley into the large bowl and stir to combine. Pour egg mixture into the prepared dish and bake for 35 minutes. Garnish with parsley and serve.

Healthy Zucchini Frittata

Cook time: 25 minutes | Serves: 6 | Per Serving: Calories 145, Carbs 4g, Fat 9g, Protein 11g

Ingredients:

- Eggs – 2
- Zucchini – 4 cups, grated
- Cheddar cheese – 1/2 cup, shredded
- Mozzarella cheese – 1 cup, shredded
- Parmesan cheese – 1/2 cup, grated
- Garlic – 1 tbsp., minced
- Onion – 1/2 cup, diced
- Salt – 1/2 tsp.

Directions:

Preheat the oven to 375 F. Grease baking dish and set aside. Add zucchini and salt into the colander and set aside for 10 minutes. After 10 minutes squeeze out all liquid from zucchini. Combine together zucchini, cheddar cheese, mozzarella cheese, 1/2 parmesan cheese, eggs, garlic, and onion and pour into the prepared dish. Bake for 25 minutes. Serve.

Cauliflower Broccoli Risotto

Cook time: 15 minutes | Serves: 2 | Per Serving: Calories 315, Carbs 11.9g, Fat 22.1g, Protein 16g

Ingredients:

- Broccoli head – 1, cut into florets
- Cauliflower head – 1, cut into florets
- Lemon zest – 1 tbsp.
- Vegetable stock – 1/2 cup
- Butter – 2 tbsps.
- Onion spring – 2, chopped
- Parmesan cheese – 1/2 cup, grated
- Cream – 2 tbsps.
- Pepper – 1/2 tsp.
- Salt – 1/2 tsp.

Directions:

Add cauliflower and broccoli florets into the food processor and process until it looks like rice. Melt butter in a saucepan over medium heat. Add onion and sauté for 2 minutes. Add broccoli and cauliflower rice and sauté for 2-3 minutes. Add stock and cover and cook for 10 minutes. Stir frequently. Add parmesan cheese and cream. Season with lemon zest. Stir until cheese is melted. Serve.

Cheesy Broccoli Casserole

Cook time: 30 minutes │Serves: 8 │ Per Serving: Calories 285, Carbs 9g, Fat 23g, Protein 12g

Ingredients:

- Broccoli florets – 2 lbs.
- Garlic cloves – 2, minced
- Cream cheese – 4 oz.
- Mozzarella cheese – 1 cup
- Cheddar cheese – 2 cups, shredded
- Vegetable stock – 1/4 cup
- Heavy cream – 1/2 cup
- Olive oil – 3 tbsps.
- Pepper & salt, to taste

Directions:

Preheat the oven to 400 F. Layer broccoli florets in a casserole dish. Drizzle with oil and season with pepper and salt. Roast broccoli in the oven for 15-20 minutes. Meanwhile, combine together heavy cream, stock, garlic, cream cheese, mozzarella cheese, and 1 cup cheddar cheese in a medium saucepan over medium-low heat. Stir frequently. Once broccoli is cooked then pour heavy cream mixture over top and mix well. Sprinkle remaining cheddar cheese on top and bake for 15 minutes more. Serve.

Spinach Mushroom Cheese Quiche

Cook time: 40 minutes │ Serves: 6 │ Per Serving: Calories 185, Carbs 4.2g, Fat 13g, Protein 13g

Ingredients:

- Eggs – 6
- Mozzarella cheese – 1 cup, shredded
- Garlic powder – 1/2 tsp.
- Parmesan cheese – 1/3 cup, shredded
- Water – 1/2 cup
- Heavy cream – 1/2 cup
- Cheese slices – 2
- Can mushroom – 8 oz., sliced
- Frozen spinach – 10 oz., thawed and drained
- Pepper & salt, to taste

Directions:

Spread spinach into a pie pan and spread mushrooms over spinach. Whisk eggs together with water and heavy cream. Mix in garlic powder, parmesan, pepper, and salt. Pour egg mixture over vegetables in pie pan. Top with shredded mozzarella cheese. Bake at 350 F for 40 minutes. Serve.

Mushrooms Spinach Pie

Cook time: 55 minutes │ Serves: 4 │ Per Serving: Calories 440, Carbs 6g, Fat 37g, Protein 21g

Ingredients:

- Eggs – 4
- Cheddar cheese – 1 1/2 cups, grated
- Cream cheese – 3 oz., softened
- Spinach leaves – 8 oz.
- Butter – 1/4 cup
- Mushrooms – 12, sliced
- Garlic – 1 tsp., minced
- Onion – 1/2., chopped

Directions:

Heat butter in a pan over medium heat. Add onion, mushrooms, and garlic and sauté until softened. Add spinach and cook until spinach is wilted. In a medium bowl, whisk eggs until frothy. Add cream cheese and whisk for a minute. Add vegetables and one cup grated cheese. Pour the mixture into a greased casserole dish and cover with the remaining cheese. Bake at 350 F for 45 minutes. Serve.

Spinach Pie

Cook time: 35 minutes │ Serves: 6 │ Per Serving: Calories 255, Carbs 2.8g, Fat 19g, Protein 17g

Ingredients:

- Eggs – 5, beaten
- Cheese – 2 1/2 cups, grated
- Frozen spinach – 10 oz., thawed, squeezed, and drained
- Garlic powder – 1/4 tsp.
- Dried onion – 1 tsp., minced
- Pepper & salt, to taste

Directions:

Spray a 9-inch pie dish with cooking spray and set aside. Add all ingredients into the mixing bowl and mix until well combined. Pour pie mixture into the prepared dish and bake at 375 F for 30 minutes. Serve.

Creamy Garlic Mushrooms

Cook time: 35 minutes | Serves: 4 | Per Serving: Calories 175, Carbs 10g, Fat 11g, Protein 6.2g

Ingredients:

- Mushrooms – 1 1/2 lbs., cleaned and quartered
- Heavy whipping cream – 1/2 cup
- Dry red wine – 1/2 cup
- Dried basil – 1 tbsp.
- Garlic cloves – 2, minced
- Onion – 1, sliced
- Butter – 2 tbsps.
- Pepper – 1/2 tsp.
- Salt – 1 1/2 tsp.

Directions:

Heat butter in a large pan over medium-high heat. Add onion and sauté for 15 minutes. Add mushrooms and season with pepper and salt and cook for 15 minutes more. Add basil and garlic and stir well. Add wine and stir well. Turn heat to low and continue to reduce wine over low heat. Add cream and stir for a minute. Serve.

Rice & Grains

Easy & Tasty French Onion Rice

Cook time: 25 minutes | Serves: 6 | Per Serving: Calories 182, Carbs 28.9g, Fat 6g, Protein 2.8g

Ingredients:

- Rice – 1 cup, rinsed
- Onion soup mix – 1 packet
- Butter – 3 tbsps.
- Vegetable stock – 3 cups.

Directions:

Add 1 tablespoon butter, rice, stock, and onion soup mix into the medium saucepan and bring to boil. Reduce heat to low and cook for 20 minutes. Fluff rice with fork. Add remaining butter and mix well. Serve.

Herb Bean Rice

Cook time: 20 minutes | Serves: 6 | Per Serving: Calories 360, Carbs 65g, Fat 5g, Protein 14g

Ingredients:

- Can black beans – 30 oz., drained
- Vegetable broth – 3 ½ cups
- Brown rice – 1 ½ cups
- Cayenne pepper – ½ tsp.
- Oregano – 1 tsp.
- Thyme – 1 tsp.
- Onion powder – 1 tsp.
- Garlic powder – 1 tsp.
- Parsley – 1 tsp.
- Tomatoes – ¼ cup, diced
- Garlic clove – 1, chopped
- Bell pepper – 1, chopped
- Onion – ½, chopped
- Olive oil – 1 tbsp.
- Pepper – ¼ tsp.
- Salt – 1 tsp.

Directions:

Cook rice in a rice cooker with broth. Heat oil in a large pan over medium heat. Add onion and bell pepper and sauté for 10 minutes. Add remaining ingredients except for rice to the pan and stir well and cook for 10 minutes. Add rice stir to combine and cook until heat through. Serve.

Delicious Rice & Beans

Cook time: 60 minutes | Serves: 6 | Per Serving: Calories 425, Carbs 69g, Fat 11g, Protein 13g

Ingredients:

- Long-grain brown rice – 2 cups
- Fresh cilantro – ¼ cup, chopped
- Can black beans – 16 oz., rinsed
- Vegetable broth – 4 cups
- Can tomatoes – 14.5 oz., diced
- Red pepper flakes – ¼ tsp.
- Ground cumin – 1 tsp.
- Garlic cloves – 2, minced
- Bell pepper – 1, diced
- Onion – 1, diced
- Olive oil – ¼ cup

Directions:

Heat oil in a large pan over medium heat. Add onion and sauté for 3-5 minutes. Add bell pepper and cook for 3-4 minutes. Add red pepper flakes, cumin, and garlic and cook for a minute. Add tomatoes and stir for 5 minutes. Add rice and broth and stir well and bring to boil. Turn heat to low, cover, and simmer for about 45 minutes or until rice is cooked. Stir in cilantro and black beans and let it rest for 5-10 minutes. Serve.

Red Pepper Bean Rice

Cook time: 20 minutes | Serves: 4 | Per Serving: Calories 350, Carbs 59g, Fat 9g, Protein 10g

Ingredients:

- Can black beans – 15 oz., drained
- Cooked brown rice – 3 cups
- Cayenne pepper – 1/8 tsp.
- Paprika – ¼ tsp.
- Cumin – ½ tsp.
- Salsa – 1/3 cup
- Garlic cloves – 2, minced
- Onion – 1, diced
- Red bell pepper – 1, diced
- Olive oil – 2 tbsps.
- Salt – ½ tsp.

Directions:

Heat oil in a large pan over medium heat. Add onion and bell peppers and sauté for 5-7 minutes. Add garlic and sauté for a minute. In a small bowl, mix together cayenne pepper, paprika, cumin, and salt. Add beans, rice, and spice mixture to the pan and stir to combine. Add salsa and stir well. Cover and cook for 5-10 minutes over low heat. Serve.

Healthy Quinoa & Vegetables

Cook time: 4 hours | Serves: 4 | Per Serving: Calories 390, Carbs 49g, Fat 14g, Protein 18g

Ingredients:

- Quinoa – 1 ½ cups, rinsed
- Basil – 1 tsp.
- Garlic cloves – 2, minced
- Fresh green beans – 1 cup, chopped
- Carrot – 1 cup, chopped
- Sweet red pepper – 1, chopped
- Olive oil – 1 tbsp.
- Onion – 1, chopped
- Vegetable stock – 3 cups
- Pepper & salt, to taste

Directions:

Add all ingredients into the slow cooker and stir everything well. Cover slow cooker with lid and cook on low for 4 hours. Fluff quinoa with a fork. Serve.

Broccoli Brown Rice Casserole

Cook time: 40 minutes | Serves: 8 | Per Serving: Calories 325, Carbs 50g, Fat 11g, Protein 9g

Ingredients:

- Broccoli florets – 3 cups
- Brown rice – 2 cups, cooked
- Garlic cloves – 2, minced
- Onion – 1, chopped
- Olive oil – 1 tbsp.
- For sauce:
- Garlic clove – 1, minced
- Tapioca starch – 1 tbsp.
- Onion – 1 tbsp., chopped
- Nutritional yeast flakes – ¼ cup
- Water – 1 cup
- Cashews – 1 cup
- Salt – 1 ½ tsp.

Directions:

Preheat the oven to 400 F. Grease 9*13-inch casserole dish and set aside. For the sauce: add all sauce ingredients into the blender and blend until smooth and creamy. Heat oil in a pan over medium-high heat. Add garlic and onion and sauté until onion is softened. Add broccoli and cook for a minute. Add rice and sauce and stir well. Transfer broccoli rice mixture into the prepared dish. Cover and bake for 35-40 minutes. Serve.

Olive Zucchini Quinoa

Cook time: 25 minutes | Serves: 4 | Per Serving: Calories 300, Carbs 41g, Fat 10g, Protein 11g

Ingredients:

- Quinoa – 1 cup, rinsed and drained
- Tomato – 1, chopped
- Can chickpeas – 3/4 cup, rinsed and drained
- Water – 2 cups
- Zucchini – 1, chopped
- Garlic – 1 tbsp., chopped
- Olive oil – 1 tbsp.
- Fresh basil – 2 tbsps., chopped
- Olives – 1/4 cup, chopped
- Feta cheese – 6 tbsps., crumbled

Directions:

Heat olive oil in a saucepan over medium-high heat. Add quinoa and garlic and cook for 2-3 minutes. Add water and zucchini and stir well. Bring to boil. Turn heat to low and simmer for 15 minutes. Add remaining ingredients and stir until heated through. Serve.

Dill Leek Rice

Cook time: 30 minutes | Serves: 4 | Per Serving: Calories 305, Carbs 35g, Fat 17g, Protein 3g

Ingredients:

- Brown rice – ½ cup, uncooked
- Hot water – 1 ¼ cup
- Tomato paste – 1 ½ tsp.
- Dill – 1 ½ tbsps., chopped
- Olive oil – 1/3 cup
- Leeks – 1 lb., sliced
- Pepper & salt, to taste

Directions:

Add sliced leek in boiling water and cook for 2-3 minutes. Strain and set aside. Heat oil in a saucepan over medium-low heat. Add leek and sauté for 5-7 minutes. Add tomato paste and dill and cook for 1-2 minutes. Add hot water, rice, pepper, and salt and stir well. Cover and simmer over low heat for 20 minutes. Serve.

Healthy Spinach Rice

Cook time: 35 minutes | Serves: 6 | Per Serving: Calories 200, Carbs 29g, Fat 8g, Protein 4g

Ingredients:

- Brown rice – 1 cup, uncooked
- Lemon zest – ½ tbsp.
- Fresh lemon juice – 1 ½ tbsps.
- Vegetable stock – 2 cups
- Baby spinach – ½ lb.
- Dill – 3 tbsps., chopped
- Green onion – 4 tbsps., chopped
- Garlic – 1 tbsp., chopped
- Onion – 1, chopped
- Olive oil – 3 tbsps.

Directions:

Heat oil in a large pot over medium-high heat. Add onion and sauté for 5 minutes. Add garlic, 2 tbsps. green onion, and 2 tbsps. dill and sauté for 2 minutes. Add spinach and cook until the spinach has wilted for about 3-4 minutes. Add rice and stock and stir well. Bring to boil. Turn heat to medium-low and simmer for 20 minutes. Stir in lemon zest, lemon juice, and remaining green onion and dill. Serve.

Chickpeas & Spinach Quinoa

Cook time: 25 minutes | Serves: 6 | Per Serving: Calories 235, Carbs 35g, Fat 7g, Protein 8g

Ingredients:

- Quinoa – 1 cup, uncooked
- Can chickpeas – 14.5 oz., drained and rinsed
- Spinach – 1 cup, chopped
- Vegetable stock – 2 cups.
- Sun-dried tomatoes – ½ cup, chopped
- Olives – ¾ cup, sliced
- Dried dill – ¼ tsp.
- Dried thyme – ¼ tsp.
- Chili flakes – ½ tsp.
- Shallot – 2 tbsps., minced
- Garlic – 1 tbsp., minced
- Olive oil – 1 tbsp.
- Pepper & Salt, to taste

Directions:

Heat olive oil in a saucepan over medium heat. Add shallot, garlic, and chili flakes and cook for 2 minutes. Add dill and thyme and cook for 30 seconds. Add quinoa, sun-dried tomatoes, and olives and stir for 30 seconds. Add stock and stir well. Bring to boil. Cover and turn heat to low and simmer for 20-25 minutes. Remove lid. Add chickpeas and spinach and stir until spinach is wilted. Season with pepper and salt. Serve.

Herb Quinoa

Cook time: 25 minutes | Serves: 6 | Per Serving: Calories 105, Carbs 18g, Fat 2g, Protein 4g

Ingredients:

- Quinoa – 1 cup
- Garlic powder – 1 tsp.
- Garlic – 1 tsp., minced
- Fresh basil – 1 tbsp., chopped
- Roasted red pepper – 1 tsp., chopped
- Fresh parsley – 1 tbsp., chopped
- Lemon juice – 1
- Lemon zest – 1
- Water – 2 cups

Directions:

Add all ingredients into the saucepan and stir well. Bring to boil. Turn heat to medium-low and simmer for 20 minutes. Remove from heat. Cover and let it sit for 5 minutes. Fluff quinoa with a fork. Serve.

Quinoa Veggie Pilaf

Cook time: 25 minutes | Serves: 4 | Per Serving: Calories 195, Carbs 32g, Fat 5g, Protein 6g

Ingredients:

- Quinoa – 1 cup, rinsed
- Baby spinach – 1 cup
- Medium tomato – 1, chopped
- Carrot – 1, peeled and chopped
- Thyme – 1 tsp.
- Pepper – ½ tsp.
- Water – 2 cups
- Small onion – 1, chopped
- Olive oil – 2 tsps.

Directions:

Heat olive oil in a saucepan over medium heat. Add onion to the pan and sauté for 5 minutes. Add quinoa and cook for 2 minutes. Add water, thyme, and black pepper and stir well. Bring to boil. Turn heat to low and simmer for 5 minutes. Add carrots and stir well. Cover the saucepan with a lid and simmer for 10 minutes. Remove saucepan from heat and add spinach and tomatoes and stir for 3 minutes. Serve.

Easy Millet Porridge

Cook time: 25 minutes | Serves: 4 | Per Serving: Calories 395, Carbs 30g, Fat 29g, Protein 6g

Ingredients:

- Hulled millet – 2/3 cup
- Water – 1 ½ cups
- Almond milk – 2 cups
- Pinch of salt

Directions:

Add millet, water, almond milk, and salt in a saucepan and bring to boil. Turn heat to low and simmer for 25 minutes. Serve.

Cilantro Lime Rice

Cook time: 5 minutes | Serves: 8 | Per Serving: Calories 155, Carbs 21g, Fat 7g, Protein 2g

Ingredients:

- Cooked brown rice – 4 cups
- Fresh lime juice – 2 tbsps.
- Olive oil – ¼ cup
- Green onion – ½ cup, chopped
- Cilantro – 1 cup
- Pepper & salt, to taste

Directions:

Add cilantro, lime juice, oil, green onion, pepper, and salt into the blender and blend until smooth. Pour cilantro mixture over cooked rice and mix well. Serve.

Tasty Tomato Rice

Cook time: 20 minutes | Serves: 4 | Per Serving: Calories 326, Carbs 64g, Fat 4g, Protein 6g

Ingredients:

- Vegetable stock – 1 ¼ cup
- Can tomatoes – 14 oz., cubed
- White rice – 10.5 oz.
- Olive oil – 1 tbsp.
- Pepper & salt, to taste

Directions:

Heat oil in a pan over medium heat. Add rice and stir well. Add tomatoes, stock, and stir well and bring to boil. Turn heat to low and simmer for 15-20 minutes. Season with pepper and salt. Serve.

Quinoa with Eggplant

Cook time: 30 minutes | Serves: 4 | Per Serving: Calories 360, Carbs 49g, Fat 14g, Protein 11g

Ingredients:

- Large eggplant – 1, cut into cubes
- Fresh spinach – 5 oz.
- Cooked quinoa – 1 1/2 cups
- Olive oil – 3 tbsps.
- Pepper & salt, to taste

Directions:

Preheat the oven to 420 F. Spray baking tray with cooking spray and set aside. In a large bowl, toss eggplant with 2 tbsps. oil. Season with pepper and salt. Spread eggplant onto baking tray and roast for 20-25 minutes. Heat remaining oil in a pan over a medium heat. Add spinach and cook until spinach is wilted. Remove pan from heat. Add roasted eggplant in spinach. Add quinoa and stir well. Serve.

Flavorful Herb Quinoa

Cook time: 15 minutes | Serves: 2 | Per Serving: Calories 315, Carbs 54g, Fat 5g, Protein 12g

Ingredients:

- Quinoa – 1 cup, rinsed
- Water – 2 cups
- Lemon zest – 1 tsp., grated
- Fresh mint – 1 ½ tsps., chopped
- Fresh cilantro – 1 tbsp., chopped
- Fresh basil – 1 tbsp., chopped
- Salt – ½ tsp.

Directions:

Add water in a saucepan and bring to boil. Add quinoa and salt to the boiling water. Cover and simmer for 12-15 minutes. Remove saucepan from heat. Fluff quinoa with a fork and add in a large bowl. Add remaining ingredients into the quinoa and stir well. Serve.

Lime Zucchini Rice

Cook time: 20 minutes | Serves: 4 | Per Serving: Calories 285, Carbs 59g, Fat 2.5g, Protein 6.2g

Ingredients:

- White rice – 1 ½ cups
- Water – 3 cups
- Lime juice – 1 tbsp.
- Olive oil – ½ tbsp.

- Cumin seeds – 1 tsp.
- Medium zucchini – 2, grated
- Pepper & salt, to taste

Directions:

Add water, rice, and salt in a medium pot and bring to boil. Turn heat to low and simmer for 15 minutes. Remove from heat and fluff rice with a fork. Heat oil in a pan over medium heat. Add cumin seeds and sauté for 30 seconds. Add zucchini and cook for 3-4 minutes. Add rice, lime juice, pepper, and salt and stir well. Serve.

Bell Pepper Tomato Rice

Cook time: 1 hour 45 minutes | Serves: 3 | Per Serving: Calories 335, Carbs 54g, Fat 11g, Protein 5g

Ingredients:

- Brown rice – 1 cup
- Tomatoes – 1 cup, chopped
- Red bell pepper – ½, diced
- Olive oil – 2 tbsps.
- Salt

Directions:

Heat oil in a saucepan over low heat. Add bell pepper and sauté for 5 minutes. Add tomatoes and stir well and cook for 5 minutes. Add rice, 2 ½ cups water, and salt and bring to simmer and cook for 5-8 minutes. Cover and cook for 25 minutes. Turn off the heat and let sit for 5 minutes. Fluff the rice using a fork. Serve.

Lentil Rice

Cook time: 24 minutes | Serves: 6 | Per Serving: Calories 260, Carbs 41g, Fat 7g, Protein 8g

Ingredients:

- Brown rice – 1 1/2 cups
- Vegetable broth – 3 1/2 cups
- Dry brown lentils – 1 cup
- Curry powder – 1 1/2 tsps.
- Ground cumin – 1 1/2 tsps.
- Garlic powder – 1/2 tbsp.
- Olive oil – 2 tbsps.
- Mushrooms – 1/2 cup, chopped
- Bell pepper – 1/2 cup, chopped
- Onion – 1/2 cup, chopped

Directions:

Add oil into the instant pot and set the pot on sauté mode. Add onion, mushrooms, and bell pepper and sauté until vegetables are softened. Add spices and stir well. Add rice, lentils, and broth and stir well. Seal pot with lid and cook on high pressure for 24 minutes. Once done, allow to release pressure naturally. Open the lid. Serve.

Tasty Mushroom Rice

Cook time: 35 minutes | Serves: 4 | Per Serving: Calories 306, Carbs 43g, Fat 11g, Protein 9g

Ingredients:

- Brown rice – 1 cup
- Chives – 1 1/2 tbsps., chopped
- Butter – 2 tbsps.
- Vegetable broth – 1 1/4 cup
- Mushrooms – 1 lb., sliced
- Dried thyme – 1/2 tsp.
- Worcestershire sauce – 1 1/2 tsps.
- Garlic cloves – 2, minced
- Onion – 1, diced
- Olive oil – 1 tbsp.
- Pepper & salt, to taste

Directions:

Add oil into the instant pot and set the pot on sauté mode. Add garlic and onion and sauté for 2-3 minutes. Add Worcestershire sauce, thyme, and mushrooms and cook for 4-5 minutes. Add broth and rice and stir well. Seal pot with lid and cook on high for 25 minutes. Once done, release pressure using quick release. Open the lid. Add butter and stir until butter is melted. Garnish with chives. Serve.

Parmesan Rice

Cook time: 23 minutes | Serves: 4 | Per Serving: Calories 280, Carbs 37g, Fat 10g, Protein 6g

Ingredients:

- Jasmine rice – 1 cup
- Parmesan cheese – 1/4 cup, shredded
- Vegetable broth – 1 cup
- Sherry – 1/2 cup
- Garlic cloves – 2, minced
- Small onion – 1/2, diced
- Butter – 3 tbsps.

Directions:

Add butter into the instant pot and set the pot on sauté mode. Add garlic, onion, and rice and stir for 2-3 minutes. Add broth and sherry and stir well. Seal pot with lid and cook on high for 20 minutes. Once done, allow to release pressure naturally. Open the lid. Fluff rice with a fork. Add cheese and stir well. Serve.

Delicious Pea Risotto

Cook time: 3 minutes | Serves: 4 | Per Serving: Calories 301, Carbs 15g, Fat 8g, Protein 10g

Ingredients:

- White rice – 1 cup, uncooked
- Asparagus – 3/4 cup, chopped
- Peas – 1 cup
- Lemon zest – 1/2 tbsp.
- Parmesan cheese – 1 cup, shredded
- Vegetable broth – 1 3/4 cups
- Garlic cloves – 2, minced
- Onion – 1/2, chopped
- Butter – 2 tbsps.

Directions:

Add butter, garlic, onion, rice, and broth into the instant pot and stir well. Seal pot with lid and cook on high for 3 minutes. Once done, release pressure using quick release. Open the lid. Stir in asparagus, peas, lemon zest, and cheese. Cover with lid and let sit for 5 minutes. Serve.

Turmeric Rice

Cook time: 7 minutes | Serves: 4 | Per Serving: Calories 190, Carbs 35g, Fat 3g, Protein 3g

Ingredients:

- Jasmine rice – 1 cup, uncooked and rinsed
- Garlic powder – 1/4 tsp.
- Turmeric – 3/4 tsp.
- Olive oil – 1 tbsp.
- Water – 1 cup
- Salt – 1/2 tsp.

Directions:

Add oil into the instant pot and set the pot on sauté mode. Add turmeric, garlic powder, rice, and salt and stir for 1-2 minutes. Add water and stir well. Seal pot with lid and cook on high for 6 minutes. Once done, allow to release pressure naturally. Open the lid. Fluff the rice with a fork. Serve.

Tasty Rice Pilaf

Cook time: 9 minutes | Serves: 4 | Per Serving: Calories 315, Carbs 42g, Fat 13g, Protein 5g

Ingredients:

- Orzo rice – 1/3 cup, uncooked
- Fresh parsley – 1 tbsp., chopped
- Paprika – 1/2 tsp.
- Onion powder – 1/4 tsp.
- Garlic powder – 1/2 tsp.
- Vegetable broth – 1 1/2 cups
- White rice – 1 cup, uncooked and rinsed
- Olive oil – 1/4 cup
- Pepper – 1/4 tsp.
- Sea salt – 3/4 tsp.

Directions:

Add oil into the pot and set the pot on sauté mode. Add orzo and cook for 2-3 minutes. Add rice and cook for 3-4 minutes. Add paprika, onion powder, garlic powder, pepper, broth, and salt and stir well. Seal pot with lid and cook on high for 3 minutes. Once done, allow to release pressure naturally. Open the lid. Serve.

Pasta & Noodles

Broccoli Spaghetti

Cook time: 1 hour 30 minutes │Serves: 6 │ Per Serving: Calories 550, Carbs 47g, Fat 30g, Protein 26g

Ingredients:

- Spaghetti – 1 lb., break into 3-inch pieces
- Parmesan cheese – ½ cup., shredded
- Mozzarella cheese – 2 cups, shredded
- Romano cheese – 1 ½ cups, grated
- Garlic cloves – 8, minced
- Broccoli florets – 12 oz.
- Olive oil – ½ cup
- Pepper & salt, to taste

Directions:

Add water and salt in an 8-quart pot and bring to boil. Add broccoli, garlic, spaghetti, pepper, and oil and stir well and boil for 2-3 minutes. Turn off the heat. Cover the pot and let it sit for one hour. Stir every 15 minutes or until pasta is cooked. Add Romano cheese and stir until cheese is melted. Add remaining cheese and stir until cheese is melted. Serve.

Easy Vegan Pasta

Cook time: 5 minutes │Serves: 6 │ Per Serving: Calories 285, Carbs 34g, Fat 12g, Protein 11g

Ingredients:

- Pasta – 10 oz.
- Walnuts – ½ cup
- Olives – ½ cup
- Garlic – 1 tbsp., minced
- Water – 1/3 cup
- Hummus – 1 cup
- Pepper & salt, to taste

Directions:

Cook pasta according to packet instructions. Meanwhile, in a mixing bowl, mix hummus, garlic, water, walnuts, olives, pepper, and salt. Once pasta is done then drained well and add in hummus mixture. Stir well and serve.

Mac n Cheese

Cook time: 20 minutes │Serves: 4 │ Per Serving: Calories 380, Carbs 41g, Fat 18g, Protein 15g

Ingredients:

- Elbow macaroni – 2 cups
- Italian seasoning – ½ tsp.
- Unsweetened almond milk – 1 cup
- Vegetable stock – 1 cup
- Mozzarella cheese – ¼ cup, shredded
- Cheddar cheese – ½ cup, cubed
- Feta cheese – ½ cup, crumbled
- Baby spinach – 8 oz.
- Tomatoes – 2, diced
- Garlic – 1 tbsp., minced
- Onion – 1, diced
- Olive oil – 2 tbsps.
- Pepper & salt, to taste

Directions:

Heat oil in a pan over medium-high heat. Add onion and sauté for 2-3 minutes. Add garlic and sauté for 30 seconds. Add tomatoes, milk, stock, macaroni, cheeses, spinach, and seasonings. Stir well and bring to boil. Turn heat to medium-low. Cover pan with lid and cook for 12-15 minutes. Stir frequently. Serve.

Caprese Pasta

Cook time: 20 minutes | Serves: 6 | Per Serving: Calories 310, Carbs 44g, Fat 10g, Protein 11g

Ingredients:

- Pasta – 1 lb.
- Mozzarella cheese – 1 ½ cups, shredded
- Garlic – 1 tbsp., minced
- Basil – ½ cup
- Cherry tomatoes – 2 cups, halved
- Olive oil – 3 tbsps.
- Water – 4 ½ cups
- Pepper & salt, to taste

Directions:

In a large pot, combine water, tomatoes, pasta, basil, garlic, oil, pepper, and salt and cook over high heat. Bring to boil. Turn heat to medium-low and simmer for 12 minutes. Remove from heat and let sit for 2-3 minutes. Add cheese and stir until cheese is melted. Season with pepper and salt. Serve.

Zucchini Noodles

Cook time: 35 minutes | Serves: 4 | Per Serving: Calories 190, Carbs 6g, Fat 15g, Protein 8g

Ingredients:

- Medium zucchini – 2, spiralized
- Butter – 2 tbsps.
- Fresh thyme – 1 tsp., chopped
- Small onion – 1, sliced
- Cheddar cheese – 1 cup, grated
- Worcestershire sauce – 2 tsps.
- Vegetable broth – 1/4 cup
- Pepper & salt, to taste

Directions:

Spray a 5*8-inch baking dish with cooking spray and set aside. Preheat the oven to 390 F. Melt butter in a pan over medium heat. Add onion and sauté until softened. Add thyme, Worcestershire sauce, pepper, and salt. Stir for minutes. Add broth in the pan and cook onions for 10 minutes. In a large bowl, mix together zucchini noodles and onion mixture and pour into the baking dish. Top with cheese and bake for 25 minutes. Garnish with thyme. Serve.

Garlic Butter Ravioli

Cook time: 15 minutes | Serves: 4 | Per Serving: Calories 475, Carbs 9g, Fat 43g, Protein 11g

Ingredients:

- Ravioli – 20 oz.
- Italian seasoning – 1 tsp.
- Olive oil – 1 tbsp.
- Garlic – 2 tbsps. , minced
- Butter – ¼ cup
- White wine – ½ cup
- Parmesan cheese – 1 ¾ cups, grated
- Heavy cream – 2 cups
- Sun-dried tomatoes – 6 oz., chopped
- Baby spinach – 2 cups

Directions:

Boil ravioli in salted water for 2-3 minutes. Drain well and set aside. Heat olive oil and butter in a large pan over medium heat. Add Italian seasoning and stir for 20 seconds. Add garlic and cook for minute. Add wine and simmer for 2-3 minutes. Stir in heavy cream. Bring to boil and simmer for 6-8 minutes. Stir frequently. Turn heat to low and add parmesan cheese and stir to combine. Stir in sun-dried tomatoes and spinach. Add cooked ravioli and stir well. Serve.

Mushroom Ravioli

Cook time: 30 minutes | Serves: 2 | Per Serving: Calories 875, Carbs 53g, Fat 58g, Protein 37g

Ingredients:

- Frozen ravioli – 12 oz.

- Dried basil – 1 tbsp.
- Parmesan cheese – ½ cup, grated
- Mushrooms – 8 oz., sliced
- Butter – 2 tbsps.
- Heavy cream – 1 cup
- Pine nuts – 2 tbsps., toasted
- Pepper & salt, to taste

Directions:

Add heavy cream in a saucepan and simmer over medium-low heat, about 15 minutes. At the same time, melt butter in a large pan over medium-high heat. Add mushrooms and cook for 10 minutes. Stir frequently. Add cream, basil, parmesan cheese, pepper, and salt in the mushrooms and stir well. Cook ravioli in a medium saucepan and drain well. Add cook ravioli in the mushroom cheese mixture and toss well. Remove pan from heat. Top with pine nuts. Serve.

Cheesy Spaghetti

Cook time: 10 minutes | Serves: 4 | Per Serving: Calories 440, Carbs 48g, Fat 20g, Protein 16g

Ingredients:

- Spaghetti – 12 oz.
- Italian cheese blend – ¾ cup, shredded
- Vegetable broth – ¾ cup
- Heavy cream – ¾ cup
- Garlic cloves – 3, minced
- Olive oil – 1 tbsp.
- Pepper & salt, to taste

Directions:

Cook spaghetti pasta in salted water until al dente. Drain well and set aside. Reserve 1 cup of pasta water. Heat oil in a pan over medium heat. Add garlic and sauté for a minute. Add ½ cup reserved pasta water, heavy cream, and broth and stir well. Add cooked spaghetti pasta and stir well. Remove pan from heat and stir in cheese. Add more reserved pasta water until sauce reached to desired consistency. Season with pepper and salt. Serve.

Parmesan Italian Spaghetti

Cook time: 15 minutes | Serves: 4 | Per Serving: Calories 395, Carbs 63g, Fat 10g, Protein 13g

Ingredients:

- Spaghetti – 1 lb.
- Parmesan cheese – 2 tbsps., grated
- Fresh parsley – 2 tbsps., chopped
- Sun-dried tomatoes – 4 tbsps., chopped
- Red chili flakes – 1 tsp.

- Garlic cloves – 3, minced
- Olive oil – 2 tbsps.
- Salt

Directions:

Cook spaghetti pasta in salted water until al dente. Drain well and set aside. Heat oil in a pan over a medium heat. Add red chili flakes, sun-dried tomatoes, and garlic and cook for 1 minute. Remove pan from heat. Add cooked pasta and parsley and stir well. Sprinkle grated parmesan cheese on top. Serve.

Spinach Spaghetti

Cook time: 15 minutes | Serves: 2 | Per Serving: Calories 495, Carbs 65g, Fat 22g, Protein 13g

Ingredients:

- Spaghetti – 9 oz., uncooked
- Lemon zest – 1 tsp.
- Lemon juice – ½.
- Spinach – 3 cups
- Coconut milk – 1 cup
- Vegetable broth – 2 ½ cups
- Garlic cloves – 3, minced
- Onion – 1, chopped
- Olive oil – 1 tbsp.
- Pepper & salt, to taste

Directions:

Heat olive oil in a large pot over medium heat. Add onion and sauté until onion is softened. Add garlic and sauté for 30 seconds. Add spaghetti, coconut milk, broth, and lemon juice. Stir for 2-3 minutes. Cook for 15 minutes. Once the spaghetti is al dente then add lemon zest and spinach. Stir well and cook for 2 minutes. Season with pepper and salt. Serve.

Garlic Pasta

Cook time: 15 minutes | Serves: 4 | Per Serving: Calories 350, Carbs 33g, Fat 17g, Protein 10g

Ingredients:

- Fettuccine pasta – ½ lb.
- Parmesan cheese – 1/3 cup., grated
- Oregano – ½ tbsp.
- Thyme – 1 tbsp.
- Butter – 2 tbsps.
- White wine – 1/3 cup
- Red pepper – ¼ tsp., crushed
- Garlic cloves – 4, minced

- Olive oil – 2 tbsps.
- Lemon juice – 2 tbsps.

Directions:

Cook fettuccine pasta in salted water until al dente. Drain well and set aside. Reserve 1 cup of pasta water. Heat oil in a pan over medium heat. Add garlic and sauté for 30 seconds. Add white wine, lemon juice, and crushed red pepper. Stir well. Turn heat to medium-high and cook until liquid reduces by half. Add oregano, thyme, butter, and 2 tablespoons of reserved pasta water and stir until butter is melted. Add lemon zest, parmesan cheese, and pasta and cook until well coated. Season with pepper and salt. Serve.

Fettuccine Pasta with Mushroom

Cook time: 25 minutes | Serves: 4 | Per Serving: Calories 630, Carbs 47g, Fat 36g, Protein 22g

Ingredients:

- Fettuccine pasta – 8 oz.
- Fresh spinach – 1 cup, chopped
- Garlic powder – ½ tsp.
- Parmesan cheese – ¾ cup, grated
- Heavy cream – 1 cup
- Vegetable broth – ½ cup
- Flour – 2 tbsps.
- Butter – ¼ cup
- Mushrooms – 8 oz., sliced
- Olive oil – 1 tbsp.
- Pepper & salt, to taste

Directions:

Cook fettuccine pasta in salted water until al dente. Drain well and set aside. Heat oil in a large pan over medium heat. Add mushrooms and cook until tender. Remove mushrooms from pan and set aside. Add butter to the pan and cook over medium-low heat. Once butter is melted then whisk in the flour and cook for a minute. Add broth, garlic powder, parmesan cheese, and heavy cream and stir well. Turn heat to medium and bring sauce to simmer for minute. Stir continuously. Turn heat to low. Season with pepper and salt. Stir in spinach and cook over low heat for 1 minute. Add fettuccine pasta and mushrooms and stir until pasta is well coated with sauce. Serve.

White Sauce Pasta

Cook time: 10 minutes | Serves: 6 | Per Serving: Calories 345, Carbs 45g, Fat 11g, Protein 15g

Ingredients:

- Penne pasta – 1 lb.
- Parmesan cheese – ½ cup, grated

- Dried parsley – 2 tsps.
- Unsweetened almond milk – 1 cup
- Vegetable broth – 1 cup
- Flour – 3 tbsps.
- Garlic – 2 tsps., minced
- Butter – 3 tbsps.
- Pepper & salt, to taste

Directions:

Cook pasta according to the packet instructions. Drain well and set aside. Melt butter in a saucepan over medium heat. Add garlic and sauté for minute. Add flour and cook for minute. Stir constantly. Add broth and milk and stir constantly until sauce thickens. Add parmesan cheese, parsley, pepper, and salt and stir until cheese is melted. Pour sauce over pasta and stir to combine. Serve.

Orzo Pasta

Cook time: 10 minutes | Serves: 6 | Per Serving: Calories 130, Carbs 12g, Fat 5g, Protein 7g

Ingredients:

- Dry orzo pasta – 2 cups
- Parmesan cheese – ½ cup, grated
- Garlic powder – ¼ tsp.
- Olive oil – 1 tbsp.
- Red pepper flakes – 1/8 tsp., crushed
- Salt – ½ tsp.

Directions:

Cook orzo pasta according to the packet instructions. Drain well and place into the large bowl. Add cheese, garlic powder, olive oil, red pepper flakes, and salt and toss well. Serve.

Garlic Butter Noodles

Cook time: 10 minutes | Serves: 4 | Per Serving: Calories 205, Carbs 16g, Fat 12g, Protein 8g

Ingredients:

- Shell pasta – 2 ¼ cups
- Garlic powder – ¼ tsp.
- Parmesan cheese – 2 tbsps., grated
- Butter – 2 tbsps., melted
- Cheddar cheese – 2/3 cup, shredded
- Pepper – 1/8 tsp.
- Salt – ¼ tsp.

Directions:

Cook pasta according to the packet directions. Add cooked pasta into the large mixing bowl. Add remaining ingredients and stir until cheese is melted. Serve.

Delicious Mac and Cheese

Cook time: 7 minutes | Serves: 4 | Per Serving: Calories 545, Carbs 21g, Fat 43g, Protein 18g

Ingredients:

- Noodles – 2 cups
- Heavy cream – 1 cup
- Vegetable stock – 1 cup
- Butter – 4 tbsps.
- Cheddar cheese – 2 cups, shredded
- Pepper & salt, to taste

Directions:

Add cream, noodles, and stock in an instant pot. Seal pot with lid and cook for 7 minutes. Release pressure using the quick-release method. Open lid carefully. Add butter, cheese, and stir until melted. Season with pepper and salt. Serve.

Pasta Salad

Cook time: 10 minutes | Serves: 2 | Per Serving: Calories 595, Carbs 82g, Fat 23g, Protein 15g

Ingredients:

- Pasta – 7.5 oz.
- Cherry tomatoes – 1 cup, halved
- For pesto:
- Lemon juice – 1 tsp.
- Olive oil – 2 tbsps.
- Pine nuts – 2 tbsps.
- Basil leaves – ¼ cup
- Pepper & salt, to taste

Directions:

Cook pasta according to the packet instructions. Add all pesto ingredients into the blender and blend until smooth. Drain pasta well and place in a large bowl. Add pesto in cooked pasta and stir well. Top with cherry tomatoes. Serve.

Spinach Avocado Pasta

Cook time: 15 minutes | Serves: 4 | Per Serving: Calories 275, Carbs 32g, Fat 14g, Protein 5g

Ingredients:

- Pasta – 2 cups

- Fresh lemon juice – 2 tbsps.
- Olive oil – 1 tbsp.
- Avocado – 1, diced
- Spinach – ¼ cup
- Pepper & salt, to taste

Directions:

Cook pasta according to packet instructions. Spray pan with cooking spray and heat over medium heat. Add spinach to the pan and sauté until wilted. Add spinach, avocado, lemon juice, oil, pepper, and salt into the blender and blend until smooth. Drain pasta well and place in a large bowl. Pour spinach mixture over pasta and toss well. Serve.

Tomato Eggplant Pasta

Cook time: 25 minutes | Serves: 4 | Per Serving: Calories 455, Carbs 75g, Fat 10g, Protein 16g

Ingredients:

- Large eggplant – 1, cut into cubes
- Tomato sauce – 2 cups
- Penne pasta – 1 lb.
- Fresh parsley – 1/4 cup, chopped
- Fresh basil – 1/4 cup, chopped
- Red chili flakes – 1/2 tsp.
- Olive oil – 2 tbsps.
- Kosher salt

Directions:

Preheat the oven to 400 F. Toss eggplant with 1 tbsp oil and spread on a baking tray and roast for 25 minutes. Cook pasta according to the packet instructions. Heat remaining oil in a pan over medium heat. Add tomato sauce, red pepper flakes, and eggplant and stir well. Drain pasta well and add to the tomato mixture and stir well. Garnish with parsley and basil. Serve.

Baked Mac & Cheese

Cook time: 20 minutes | Serves: 4 | Per Serving: Calories 400, Carbs 25g, Fat 25g, Protein 18g

Ingredients:

- Elbow macaroni – 1 1/2 cups
- Garlic powder – 1/4 tsp.
- Dry mustard – 1 tsp.
- Cheddar cheese – 8 oz., shredded
- Heavy cream – 1/2 cup
- Water – 1 cup
- Pepper & salt, to taste

Directions:

Spray a 7-inch baking dish with cooking spray. Add macaroni, garlic powder, dry mustard, cheese, heavy cream, water, pepper, and salt into the prepared baking dish and stir well. Bake at 360 F for 20 minutes. Serve.

Vegetable Pasta

Cook time: 4 minutes | Serves: 3 | Per Serving: Calories 325, Carbs 62g, Fat 5g, Protein 11g

Ingredients:

- Vegetable stock – 1 cup
- Bell pepper – 1/2, chopped
- Spinach – 1 cup, chopped
- Tomato – 1/2, diced
- Medium yellow squash – 1/2, chopped
- Small onion – 1/2, diced
- Pasta sauce – 12 oz.
- Spiral pasta – 6 oz.

Directions:

Add vegetables, pasta sauce, and stock and stir well. Seal pot with lid and cook on high for 4 minutes. Allow to release pressure naturally, Open the lid. Stir well and serve.

Creamy Veggie Pasta

Cook time: 4 minutes | Serves: 3 | Per Serving: Calories 750, Carbs 98g, Fat 21g, Protein 27g

Ingredients:

- Ziti pasta – 16 oz.
- Vegetable broth – 2 cups
- White wine – 1 cup
- Garlic cloves – 3, minced
- Peas – 1 cup
- Zucchini – 2 cups, chopped
- Heavy cream – 1 cup
- Mozzarella cheese – 1 cup

Directions:

Add pasta, garlic, vegetables, broth, and white wine into the instant pot and stir well. Seal pot with lid and cook on high for 4 minutes. Release pressure using the quick-release method. Open the lid. Set pot on sauté mode. Add heavy cream and cheese and stir until cheese is melted. Serve.

Delicious Parmesan Pasta

Cook time: 5 minutes | Serves: 3 | Per Serving: Calories 450, Carbs 43g, Fat 21g, Protein 22g

Ingredients:

- Pasta – 8 oz.
- Parsley – 2 tbsps., chopped
- Parmesan cheese – 4 oz., grated
- Water – 1/2 cup
- Heavy cream – 1/2 cup
- Vegetable broth – 1/2 cup
- Garlic clove – 1, minced
- Butter – 1 tbsp.

Directions:

Add butter into the instant pot and set pot on sauté mode. Once butter is melted then add garlic and stir for 30 seconds. Add pasta, water, heavy cream, and broth. Stir well. Seal pot with lid and cook on high for 3 minutes. Release pressure using the quick-release method. Open the lid. Add cheese and stir until cheese is melted. Garnish with parsley. Serve.

Creamy Alfredo

Cook time: 6 minutes | Serves: 4 | Per Serving: Calories 280, Carbs 7g, Fat 22g, Protein 11g

Ingredients:

- Dry linguine noodles – 1/2 lb., break in half
- Parmesan cheese – 3/4 cup, shredded
- Garlic – 1 tsp., minced
- Heavy cream – 1 1/2 cups
- Vegetable broth – 1 1/2 cups
- Pepper & salt, to taste

Directions:

Add vegetable broth, heavy cream, garlic, pepper, salt, and noodles to the instant pot. Seal pot with lid and cook on high for 6 minutes. Release pressure using the quick release method. Open the lid. Add parmesan cheese and stir until cheese melted. Serve.

Creamy Pasta Salad

Cook time: 5 minutes | Serves: 8 | Per Serving: Calories 182, Carbs 22g, Fat 8g, Protein 4g

Ingredients:

- Pasta – 1/2 lb.
- Sweet onion – 1/2, sliced
- Cucumber – 1, seeded and sliced
- For dressing:
- White vinegar – 2 tbsps.
- Fresh dill – 2 tbsps.

- Sugar – 1 tsp.
- Mayonnaise – 1/2 cup
- Sour cream – 1/2 cup
- Salt – 1/2 tsp.

Directions:

In a small bowl, whisk together all dressing ingredients. Cook pasta according to the packet instructions and drain well. Add pasta and remaining all salad ingredients into the large bowl and toss well. Pour dressing over salad and toss well. Serve.

Beans, Soy, Legumes

Green Beans & Chickpeas

Cook time: 10 minutes | Serves: 4 | Per Serving: Calories 290, Carbs 54g, Fat 2g, Protein 12g

Ingredients:

- Can chickpeas – 3 cups
- Corn-flour – 1 tbsp.
- Green beans – 7 oz., trimmed
- Garlic cloves – 2, minced
- For sauce:
- Water – ½ cup
- Tomato paste – 1 tbsp
- Rice vinegar – ¼ cup
- Tamari – ¼ cup
- Maple syrup – 2 tbsps.

Directions:

Spray pan with cooking spray and heat over medium heat. Add garlic and sauté for 2 minutes. Add green beans and sauté for 3 minutes. Meanwhile, in a small bowl, whisk together all sauce ingredients. Add chickpeas, sauce, and corn-flour to the pan and cook over medium-low heat for 5 minutes. Serve.

Beans with Swiss Chard

Cook time: 10 minutes | Serves: 6 | Per Serving: Calories 175, Carbs 21g, Fat 7g, Protein 8.2g

Ingredients:

- Can Great Northern beans – 15.5 oz, drained & rinsed
- Garlic cloves – 2, minced
- Olive oil – 3 tbsps.
- Swiss chard – 2 lbs., wash & chopped
- Pepper & salt, to taste

Directions:

Add Swiss chard into the boiling water and boil until wilted. Drain well and set aside. Heat oil in a pan over medium heat. Add garlic and beans and sauté for 30 seconds. Add Swiss chard and stir well. Season with pepper and salt. Serve.

Lentil Bean Chili

Cook time: 40 minutes | Serves: 6 | Per Serving: Calories 375, Carbs 61g, Fat 7g, Protein 20g

Ingredients:

- Can tomatoes – 28 oz, diced
- Red lentils – 1 cup
- Can kidney beans – 15 oz, drained and rinsed
- Can black beans – 15 oz, drained and rinsed
- Bay leaves – 2
- Paprika – 1 tsp.
- Cumin – 2 tsps.
- Chili powder – 2 ½ tbsps.
- Coconut sugar – 1 tsp.
- Coconut oil – 2 tbsps.
- Red bell pepper – 1, chopped
- Celery stalks – 2, diced
- Corn – 1 cup
- Onion – 1, chopped
- Garlic – 1 tbsp., minced
- Vegetable broth – 2 ½ cups.
- Pepper – ¼ tsp.
- Sea salt – ½ tsp.

Directions:

Heat oil in a pan over a medium heat. Add onion and sauté for 10 minutes. Add garlic, bell pepper, and celery and sauté for 5 minutes. Add bay leaves, coconut sugar, spices, and salt and mix well. Add all remaining ingredients and stir everything well. Bring to boil. Turn heat to low, cover, and simmer for 25 minutes. Stir well and serve.

Healthy Bean Salad

Cook time: 10 minutes | Serves: 4 | Per Serving: Calories 210, Carbs 22g, Fat 11g, Protein 7g

Ingredients:

- Cooked cannellini beans – 15 oz.
- Cooked black beans – 15 oz.
- Cooked kidney beans – 15 oz.
- Fresh parsley – ¼ cup, chopped
- Onion – 1/2, chopped
- Celery rib – 1, chopped
- For dressing:
- Garlic cloves – 2, minced
- Cumin powder – ½ tsp.
- Fresh lemon juice – 1 tbsp.
- Olive oil – 3 tbsps.
- Salt – ½ tsp.

Directions:

In a small bowl, mix together all dressing ingredients. In a mixing bowl, add beans, parsley, onion, and celery and mix well. Pour dressing over salad and toss well. Serve.

Spicy & Tasty Lentils

Cook time: 20 minutes | Serves: 2 | Per Serving: Calories 405, Carbs 59g, Fat 8g, Protein 25g

Ingredients:

- Brown lentils – 1 cup, soaked overnight
- Garlic clove – 1, sliced
- Marjoram – 1 tsp.
- Turmeric – 1 tsp.
- Olive oil – 1 tbsp.
- Cumin – 1 tsp.
- Chili powder – 1 tsp.
- Salt – 1/2 tsp.

Directions:

In a saucepan, add lentils, 2 cups water, and salt and cook over medium heat. Bring to boil. Turn heat to low and simmer for 10 minutes. Add marjoram, chili, turmeric, and garlic and stir well. Remove saucepan from heat and add oil. Stir well. Serve.

Garlicky Chickpeas

Cook time: 35 minutes | Serves: 4 | Per Serving: Calories 185, Carbs 31g, Fat 3g, Protein 9g

Ingredients:

- Chickpeas – 1 cup, dried & rinsed
- Water – 4 cups
- Bay leaves – 2
- Garlic cloves – 4
- Salt

Directions:

Add to the instant pot. Add bay leaves, salt, garlic, and water. Stir well. Seal pot with a lid and select beans mode and set timer for 35 minutes. Once done, allow releasing pressure naturally. Open the lid. Serve.

Mexican Beans & Rice

Cook time: 1 hour 30 minutes | Serves: 2 | Per Serving: Calories 345, Carbs 70g, Fat 0.2g, Protein 10g

Ingredients:

- Jalapeno – 1/2., remove seed and minced
- Garlic clove – 1, minced

- Vegetable broth – 1/2 cup
- Taco seasoning – 1 packet
- Can black beans – 7 oz.
- Jar salsa – 1/2
- Rice – 1/2 cup, uncooked

Directions:

Add all ingredients to the slow cooker and stir well. Cover with lid and cook on high for 1 1/2 hours. Stir well serve.

Lentil Squash Curry

Cook time: 8 hours | Serves: 8 | Per Serving: Calories 285, Carbs 34g, Fat 12g, Protein 12g

Ingredients:

- Red lentils – 2 cups, dried
- Vegetable stock – 3 cups
- Can tomatoes – 19 oz.
- Coconut milk – 14 oz.
- Ground cumin – 2 tsps.
- Turmeric – 2 tsps.
- Garam masala – 2 tsps.
- Ground coriander – 2 tsps.
- Curry powder – 1 tbsp.
- Fresh ginger – 2 tbsps., minced
- Garlic cloves – 2, minced
- Onion – 1, chopped
- Butternut squash – 4 cups, peel, remove seeds and diced
- Salt – 1 tsp.

Directions:

Add all ingredients into the slow cooker and cook on low for 8 hours. Mash everything using a masher and serve.

Sweet Potato Bean Curry

Cook time: 1 hour 30 minutes | Serves: 6 | Per Serving: Calories 480, Carbs 94g, Fat 2g, Protein 21g

Ingredients:

- Dry white beans – 2 cups
- Curry powder – 1 tbsp.
- Garlic cloves – 2, minced
- Onion – 1/2, diced
- Sweet potato – 1, peeled and sliced
- Water – 10 cups

- Coriander powder – 1 tsp.
- Red pepper flakes – 1 tsp.
- Brown rice – 2 cups
- Salt – 1 tbsp.

Directions:

Add all ingredients into the instant pot and stir well. Seal pot with a lid and select stew mode and set timer for 1 hour 30 minutes. Once done, allow to release pressure naturally then open the lid. Stir and serve.

Tasty Black Garbanzo Beans

Cook time: 31 minutes | Serves: 6 | Per Serving: Calories 66, Carbs 8g, Fat 3g, Protein 2g

Ingredients:

- Dried black garbanzo beans – 1 cup
- Cayenne pepper – 1/2 tsp.
- Garam masala – 1 tsp.
- Turmeric – 1/2 tsp.
- Ginger – 2 tsps., minced
- Cumin seeds – 1/2 tsp.
- Bay leaves – 2
- Water – 4 cups
- Salt – 1 tsp.
- Lemon juice – 1
- Olive oil – 1 tbsp.

Directions:

Add chickpeas, bay leaves, water, and salt into the instant pot and stir well. Seal pot with lid and cook on high for 30 minutes. Once done, allow to release pressure naturally then open the lid. Drain water and transfer cooked chickpeas in a bowl. Add oil into the instant pot and set pot on sauté mode. Add cumin seeds and sauté for 30 seconds. Add ginger and sauté for 30 seconds. Add cooked chickpeas along with remaining ingredients and stir well. Serve.

Red Beans Rice

Cook time: 8 hours | Serves: 8 | Per Serving: Calories 345, Carbs 45g, Fat 15g, Protein 9g

Ingredients:

- Dried red beans – 1 cup, soaked for overnight
- Rice – 1 ½ cups, rinsed
- Allspice – ¼ tsp.
- Red pepper flakes – 1 tsp.
- Ground ginger – ½ tsp.
- Thyme – ½ tsp.

- Lime juice – 1
- Coconut milk – 2 cups
- Vegetable stock – 3 cups
- Garlic cloves – 2, minced
- Salt – ½ tsp.

Directions:

Drain beans and place them into the large pot. Add water and bring to boil for 10-15 minutes. Drain beans and add them to the slow cooker. Add remaining ingredients into the slow cooker and stir well. Cover and cook on low for 6-8 hours. Serve.

Easy Baked Beans

Cook time: 8 minutes │Serves: 4 │ Per Serving: Calories 195, Carbs 39g, Fat 2g, Protein 8g

Ingredients:

- Can northern beans – 7.5 oz., rinsed and drained
- Can pinto beans – 7.5 oz., rinsed and drained
- Can kidney beans – 7.5 oz., rinsed and drained
- Water – 6 tbsp
- Ketchup – 1/4 cup
- Onion – 1/2, diced
- Chili powder – 1/2 tsp.
- Mustard – 1/2 tbsp.
- Brown sugar – 1/4 cup

Directions:

Add all ingredients into the instant pot and stir well. Seal pot with lid and cook on high for 8 minutes. Once done, allow to release pressure naturally then open the lid. Stir and serve.

White Bean Salad

Cook time: 20 minutes │Serves: 3 │ Per Serving: Calories 185, Carbs 25g, Fat 4g, Protein 9g

Ingredients:

- Can cannellini beans – 15 oz., rinsed
- Small onion – 1/4, sliced
- Fresh thyme – 1 tsp.
- Vinegar – 1 tbsp.
- Bell pepper – 1/2, chopped
- Dijon mustard – 1 tsp.
- Olive oil – 1 tbsp.
- Pepper & salt, to taste

Directions:

Add beans into the instant pot and season with pepper and salt. Seal pot with lid and cook on high pressure for 20 minutes. Once done, allow to release pressure naturally then open the lid. Add remaining ingredients and stir well. Serve.

Southwest Beans

Cook time: 40 minutes │Serves: 4 │ Per Serving: Calories 285, Carbs 34g, Fat 8g, Protein 20g

Ingredients:

- Dry black beans – 1 cup, rinsed
- Vegetable broth – 3 cups
- Coriander powder – 1/2 tsp.
- Chili powder – 1 tsp.
- Small onion – 1/2, diced
- Olive oil – 1 tbsp.
- Pepper – 1/4 tsp.
- Oregano – 1 tsp.
- Paprika – 1/2 tsp.
- Cumin – 2 tsps.
- Bay leaf – 1
- Garlic cloves – 3, minced
- Kosher salt – 1/4 tsp.

Directions:

Add oil into the instant pot and set pot on sauté mode. Add onion and sauté for 5 minutes or until softened. Add garlic, coriander powder, chili powder, oregano, paprika, cumin, bay leaf, pepper, and salt. Stir well. Add broth and beans and stir well. Seal pot with lid and cook on high for 35 minutes. Once done, allow to release pressure naturally then open the lid. Stir and serve.

Healthy Black Eyed Peas

Cook time: 10 minutes │Serves: 6 │ Per Serving: Calories 54, Carbs 10g, Fat 0.6g, Protein 3g

Ingredients:

- Dried black-eyed peas – 1 cup, rinsed and drained
- Liquid smoke – 1 tsp.
- Hot sauce – 1 tsp.
- Apple cider vinegar – 2 tbsps.
- Thyme – 1 tsp.
- Garlic cloves – 6, minced
- Onion – 1, chopped
- Collard greens – 4 cups, cut into pieces
- Bay leaves – 2
- Red pepper flakes – 1 tsp.
- Water – 2 cups

- Pepper – 1 tsp.
- Salt – 1 tsp.

Directions:

Add all ingredients except vinegar, liquid smoke, and hot sauce into the instant pot and stir well. Seal pot with lid and cook on high pressure for 10 minutes. Once done, allow to release pressure naturally then open the lid. Add hot sauce, liquid smoke, and vinegar and stir well. Serve.

Chili Garlic Pinto Beans

Cook time: 55 minutes | Serves: 12 | Per Serving: Calories 150, Carbs 24g, Fat 1g, Protein 10g

Ingredients:

- Dry pinto beans – 1 lb., rinsed and drained
- Onion powder – 2 tsps.
- Garlic cloves – 2, minced
- Vegetable broth – 5 cups
- Pepper – 1 tsp.
- Chili powder – 1 tsp.
- Salt – 2 tsp.

Directions:

Add all ingredients into the instant pot and stir well. Seal pot with a lid and select manual and set timer for 55 minutes. Once done, release pressure using the quick-release method. Open the lid. Serve.

Spicy Black Beans

Cook time: 40 minutes | Serves: 4 | Per Serving: Calories 239, Carbs 33g, Fat 5g, Protein 14g

Ingredients:

- Dry black beans – 1 cup, rinsed and drained
- Garlic cloves – 3, minced
- Olive oil – 1 tbsp.
- Onion – 1/2, diced
- Chipotle powder – 1 tsp.
- Paprika – 1 tsp.
- Cumin powder – 2 tsps.
- Vegetable broth – 3 cups

Directions:

Add oil into the instant pot and set pot on sauté mode. Add garlic and onion and sauté for 5 minutes. Add broth, water, spices, and black beans. Stir well. Seal pot with a lid and select

Bean/chili mode and set timer for 35 minutes. Once done, allow to release pressure naturally. Open the lid. Serve.

Tomatillo Beans

Cook time: 40 minutes | Serves: 6 | Per Serving: Calories 225, Carbs 44g, Fat 0.2g, Protein 13g

Ingredients:

- Dry great northern beans – 1 1/2 cups, soaked in water for overnight, rinsed and drained
- Onion – 1 cup, chopped
- Poblano – 1 cup, remove seeds and chopped
- Tomatillos – 2 cup, chopped
- Dried oregano – 2 tsps.
- Water – 1 1/2 cups
- Ground cumin – 1 1/2 tsps.
- Jalapeno – 1/2, chopped
- Pepper & salt, to taste

Directions:

Add tomatillos, jalapeno, onion, and poblano into the blender and blend until a chunky consistency is achieved. Pour blended vegetables into the instant pot and set pot on sauté mode. Add ground cumin and stir well. Sauté the vegetable mixture for 4-5 minutes. Add beans, oregano, and water. Stir well. Seal pot with lid and cook on high pressure for 35 minutes. Once done, allow to release pressure naturally. Open the lid. Season with pepper and salt. Serve.

Black Bean Chili

Cook time: 13 minutes | Serves: 4 | Per Serving: Calories 180, Carbs 32g, Fat 0.5g, Protein 8g

Ingredients:

- Water – 1 cup
- Jalapeno pepper – 1, minced
- Chili powder – 2 tbsps.
- Garlic cloves – 2, minced
- Dried oregano – 1 tsp.
- Bell pepper – 1, diced
- Onion – 1, diced
- Can tomatoes – 15 oz., crushed
- Can black beans – 15 oz., drained
- Ground cumin – 2 tsps.
- Olive oil – 2 tsps.
- Kosher salt – 1 tsp.

Directions:

Add oil into the instant pot and set pot on sauté mode. Add onion, oregano, and bell pepper and sauté for 7 minutes. Add garlic, cumin, and chili powder and stir for a minute. Add beans, jalapeno, tomatoes, water, and salt. Stir well. Seal pot with lid and cook on high pressure for 5 minutes. Once done, release pressure using the quick-release method. Open the lid. Stir and serve.

Lime Black Beans

Cook time: 50 minutes | Serves: 6 | Per Serving: Calories 250, Carbs 44g, Fat 2g, Protein 14g

Ingredients:

- Dry black beans – 2 cups, rinsed and drained
- Water – 3 cups
- Olive oil – 2 tsps.
- Onion – 1, chopped
- Paprika – 1 tsp.
- Chili powder – 1 tbsp.
- Garlic cloves – 4, minced
- Fresh lime juice – 1
- Salt – 1 tsp.

Directions:

Add oil into the instant pot and set pot on sauté mode. Add onion and garlic and sauté until onion is softened. Add beans, paprika, chili powder, water, and salt. Stir well. Seal pot with lid and cook on manual mode for 50 minutes. Once done, allow to release pressure naturally. Open the lid. Add lime juice and stir. Serve.

Baked Beans

Cook time: 1 hour 15 minutes | Serves: 10 | Per Serving: Calories 290, Carbs 59g, Fat 2g, Protein 10g

Ingredients:

- Dry navy beans – 1 lb., rinsed and drained
- Garlic cloves – 4, minced
- Olive oil – 1 tbsp.
- Apple cider vinegar – 2 tbsps.
- Ketchup – 3/4 cup
- Brown sugar – 1/2 cup
- Onion – 1, chopped
- Hot sauce – 2 tsps.
- Worcestershire sauce – 1 1/2 tbsp.
- Molasses – 3/4 cup
- Salt – 3/4 tsp.

Directions:

Add water and beans into the instant pot. Seal pot with a lid and select bean mode and set timer for 60 minutes. Once done, allow to release pressure naturally. Open the lid. Drain beans and set aside. Add oil into the instant pot and set pot on sauté mode. Add garlic and onion and sauté for 2-3 minutes. Add cooked beans and remaining ingredients into the instant pot and stir well. Seal pot with lid and cook on high for 15 minutes. Once done, allow to release pressure naturally. Open the lid. Stir and serve.

Flavorful Pinto Beans

Cook time: 28 minutes | Serves: 8 | Per Serving: Calories 275, Carbs 5g, Fat 5g, Protein 15g

Ingredients:

- Dry pinto beans – 1 lb., soaked overnight, rinsed and drained
- Bay leaves – 2
- Pepper – 1 tsp.
- Oregano – 1 tsp.
- Garlic – 2 tsps., minced
- Jalapeno pepper – 1, diced
- Bell pepper – 1, seeded and chopped
- Onion – 1 cup, chopped
- Cumin – 1 tsp.
- Mustard – 1 tbsp.
- Chili powder – 2 tbsps.
- Can tomato sauce – 8 oz.
- Vegetable broth – 3 1/2 cups
- Olive oil – 2 tbsps.
- Salt – 1/2 tsp.

Directions:

Add oil into the instant pot and set pot on sauté mode. Add onion, jalapeno, and bell pepper and sauté for 2-3 minutes. Add garlic and sauté for a minute. Add remaining ingredients and stir well. Seal pot with lid and cook on high for 25 minutes. Once done, allow to release pressure naturally. Open the lid. Stir and serve.

Tasty Refried Beans

Cook time: 12 minutes | Serves: 8 | Per Serving: Calories 215, Carbs 37g, Fat 1g, Protein 13g

Ingredients:

- Pinto beans – 16 oz., soaked overnight in water, rinsed and drained
- Onion – 1, diced
- Jalapeno pepper – 2, chopped
- Vegetable broth – 16 oz.
- Cilantro – 3 tsps., chopped

- Cumin – 1 tbsp.
- Cayenne – 2 tsps.
- Salt – 1 tsp.

Directions:

Add all ingredients into the instant pot and stir well. Seal pot with lid and cook on high for 12 minutes. Once done, allow to release pressure naturally. Open the lid. Mash beans mixture using masher until smooth. Serve.

Easy Black Beans

Cook time: 50 minutes | Serves: 12 | Per Serving: Calories 130, Carbs 23g, Fat 0.6g, Protein 8.2g

Ingredients:

- Dry black beans – 1 lb., rinsed
- Garlic powder – 1/2 tsp.
- Water – 5 1/2 cups
- Paprika – 1/2 tsp.
- Cumin – 1/2 tsp.
- Coriander – 1/2 tsp.

Directions:

Add all ingredients into the instant pot and stir well. Seal pot with lid and cook on high pressure for 50 minutes. Allow to release pressure naturally. Open the lid. Stir well and serve.

Nutritious Yellow Split Peas

Cook time: 3 hours 5 minutes | Serves: 2 | Per Serving: Calories 265, Carbs 37g, Fat 1g, Protein 13g

Ingredients:

- Yellow split peas – 1/2 cup, soaked in water for 1 hour
- Ground coriander seeds – 1/2 tsp.
- Garlic cloves – 2, sliced
- Medium onion – 1/2, chopped
- Mustard seeds – 1/4 tsp.
- Cumin seeds – 1/4 tsp.
- Cilantro – 2 tbsps., minced
- Cayenne – 1/8 tsp.
- Ground turmeric – 1/8 tsp.
- Olive oil – 1 tbsp.
- Tomatoes – 1 1/2, diced
- Water – 1 1/2 cups

Directions:

Add yellow split peas, salt, and water into the slow cooker. Cover with lid and cook on high for 3 hours. Heat oil in the pan over medium heat. Add cumin seeds and mustard seeds and cook for 30 seconds. Add remaining ingredients and sauté for 4 minutes. Transfer pan mixture to the slow cooker and stir well. Serve.

Bread, Muffins, Pizza

Easy Flatbread Pizza

Cook time: 10 minutes | Serves: 3 | Per Serving: Calories 195, Carbs 23g, Fat 7g, Protein 9g

Ingredients:

- Pita flatbread – 1
- Italian blend seasoning – 1/8 tsp.
- Red pepper flakes – 1/8 tsp.
- Cherry tomatoes – ½ cup, halved
- Mozzarella cheese – ½ cup, grated
- Pizza sauce – 3 tbsps.

Directions:

Preheat the oven to 350 F. Spread pizza sauce, cheese, and cherry tomatoes over flatbread. Sprinkle with red pepper flakes and Italian seasoning. Bake in a preheated oven for 10 minutes. Serve.

Spinach Cheese Flatbread Pizza

Cook time: 20 minutes | Serves: 3 | Per Serving: Calories 365, Carbs 24g, Fat 24g, Protein 14g

Ingredients:

- Garlic naan flatbread – 1
- Crushed red pepper flakes – 1/8 tsp.
- Pesto – 2 tsps.
- Feta cheese – 2 tbsps., crumbled
- Mozzarella cheese – 2 oz., grated
- Parmesan cheese – ¼ cup, grated
- Heavy cream – ¼ cup
- Garlic clove – 1, minced
- Butter – 1 tbsp.
- Fresh spinach – 5 oz., chopped
- Salt – 1/8 tsp.

Directions:

Preheat the oven to 350 F. Melt butter in a deep pan over medium-high heat. Add spinach and garlic and sauté until spinach is wilted. Add parmesan cheese, heavy cream, and salt and turn heat to low and simmer until thickened, about 5 minutes. Stir frequently. Remove pan from heat and allow to cool. Spread spinach mixture on flatbread and top with feta cheese and mozzarella cheese. Drizzle with pesto and bake in a preheated oven for 12 minutes. Serve.

Delicious Cheese Bread

Cook time: 35 minutes | Serves: 12 | Per Serving: Calories 202, Carbs 17.6g, Fat 11.9g, Protein 6.2g

Ingredients:

- Eggs – 2
- All-purpose flour – 2 cups
- Butter – ½ cup, melted
- Buttermilk – 1 cup
- Baking soda – ½ tsp.
- Baking powder – ½ tsp.
- Sugar – 1 tsp.
- Cheddar cheese – 1 cup, shredded
- Salt– ½ tsp.

Directions:

Preheat the oven for 350 F. In a large mixing bowl, mix flour, baking soda, baking powder, sugar, cheese, pepper, and salt. In a small bowl, beat eggs with buttermilk, and butter. Add egg mixture to the flour mixture and mix well. Transfer mixture into the greased 9*5-inch loaf pan and bake in preheated oven for 35-40 minutes. Allow to cool for 15 minutes. Slice and serve.

Strawberry Bread

Cook time: 60 minutes │Serves: 10 │ Per Serving: Calories 364, Carbs 40.1g, Fat 21.g, Protein 4.2g

Ingredients:

- Eggs – 2
- All-purpose flour – 2 cups
- Vanilla – 1 tsp.
- Vegetable oil – ½ cup
- Baking soda – 1 tsp.
- Cinnamon – ½ tsp.
- Brown sugar – ¼ cup
- White sugar – ½ cup
- Fresh strawberries – 2 ¼ cups, chopped
- Salt – ½ tsp.

Directions:

Preheat the oven to 350 F. Grease 9*5-inch loaf pan and set aside. In a mixing bowl, mix together flour, baking soda, cinnamon, brown sugar, white sugar, and salt. In a separate bowl, beat eggs, vanilla, and oil. Stir in strawberries. Add flour mixture to the egg mixture and stir until well combined. Pour batter into the prepared loaf pan and bake in preheated oven for 50-60 minutes. Allow to cool for 10-15 minutes. Slice and serve.

Moist Banana Bread

Cook time: 60 minutes │Serves: 6 │ Per Serving: Calories 388, Carbs 54.6g, Fat 17.3g, Protein 5.9g

Ingredients:

- Eggs – 2
- Baking powder – 1 tsp.
- Sugar – ½ cup
- Vanilla – 1 tsp.
- Butter – ½ cup, melted
- Ripe bananas – 3
- All-purpose flour – 1 ½ cups
- Pinch of salt

Directions:

Preheat the oven to 350 F. In a large bowl, add bananas and mash until smooth. Add eggs, vanilla, butter, and mix well. Add flour, baking powder, sugar, and salt and mix until well combined. Pour batter into the greased loaf pan and bake in a preheated oven for 60 minutes. Slice and serve.

Jalapeno Cheese Bread

Cook time: 60 minutes | Serves: 8 | Per Serving: Calories 276, Carbs 29.6g, Fat 12.9g, Protein 9.9g

Ingredients:

- Egg – 1
- Flour – 2 cups
- Jalapeno pepper – 1, minced
- Cheddar cheese – 1 ¼ cups, shredded
- Butter – ¼ cup, melted
- Milk – ¼ cup
- Yogurt – ¾ cup
- Sugar – 2 tbsps.
- Baking soda – ½ tsp.
- Baking powder– 1 ½ tsp.
- Salt – ½ tsp.

Directions:

Preheat the oven to 350 F. In a bowl, mix together flour, sugar, baking soda, baking powder, and salt. In a separate bowl, whisk together egg, milk, butter, and yogurt. Add egg mixture into the flour mixture and mix until well combined. Stir in jalapeno, and shredded cheese. Pour batter into the parchment-lined 9*5-inch baking tin and bake for 1 hour. Allow to cool for 10-15 minutes. Slice and serve.

Healthy Carrot Muffins

Cook time: 35 minutes | Serves: 12 | Per Serving: Calories 155, Carbs 22g, Fat 6g, Protein 2g

Ingredients:

- Shredded carrots – 2 cups
- Nutmeg – ½ tsp.

- Baking powder – 1 tsp.
- Vanilla – 2 tsps.
- Ground cinnamon – 2 tsps.
- Maple syrup – ¼ cup
- Coconut oil – ¼ cup, melted
- Applesauce – ¼ cup
- Flax meal – ¼ cup
- Old fashioned oats – ¼ cup
- Unsweetened almond milk – 1 cup
- Whole wheat flour – 1 ½ cups
- Ground ginger – ½ tsp.
- Salt – ½ tsp.

Directions:

Preheat the oven to 350 F. Spray muffin pan with cooking spray and set aside. In a mixing bowl, mix flour, ginger, nutmeg, cinnamon, baking powder, flax meal, oats, and salt. In a large bowl, whisk together almond milk, maple syrup, vanilla, coconut milk, and applesauce. Add flour mixture into the almond milk mixture and mix until combined. Add shredded carrots and stir well. Pour batter into the prepared muffin pan and bake for 30-35 minutes. Serve.

Choco Peanut Butter Muffins

Cook time: 20 minutes | Serves: 12 | Per Serving: Calories 175, Carbs 17g, Fat 11g, Protein 6g

Ingredients:

- Peanut butter – 1 cup
- Baking soda – 1 tsp.
- Vanilla – 1 tsp.
- Maple syrup – ½ cup
- Cocoa powder – ½ cup
- Applesauce – 1 cup

Directions:

Preheat the oven to 350 F. Add all ingredients into the blender and blend until smooth. Pour blended mixture into the 12 silicone muffin molds and bake for 20 minutes. Serve.

Easy Blueberry Muffins

Cook time: 25 minutes | Serves: 8 | Per Serving: Calories 345, Carbs 9g, Fat 32g, Protein 9g

Ingredients:

- Eggs – 4
- Blueberries – 1/2 cup
- Vanilla – 1 tsp.
- Heavy whipping cream – 1/2 cup

- Coconut oil – 1/2 cup, melted
- Baking powder – 1 tsp.
- Swerve – 3 tbsps.
- Almond flour – 2 cups
- Lemon juice – 1 tbsp.

Directions:

In a large bowl, whisk eggs with lemon juice, vanilla, heavy cream, and oil. In a separate bowl, mix together almond flour, swerve, and baking powder. Add almond flour mixture to the egg mixture and mix until combined. Add blueberries and fold well. Pour batter in a greased muffin tray and bake at 350 F for 20-25 minutes. Serve.

Vanilla Banana Muffins

Cook time: 15 minutes | Serves: 12 | Per Serving: Calories 125, Carbs 24g, Fat 1.4, Protein 4g

Ingredients:

- Eggs – 3
- Bananas – 3, mashed
- Applesauce – 4 tbsps.
- Honey – 1 tbsp.
- Vanilla – 1 tbsp.
- Baking soda – 1 tsp.
- Almond flour – 2 cups
- Salt – 1/2 tsp.

Directions:

Preheat the oven to 350 F. Spray muffin pan with cooking spray and set aside. In a mixing bowl, whisk together eggs, vanilla, applesauce, honey, and bananas. In a separate bowl, mix together almond flour, baking soda, and salt. Add flour mixture into the egg mixture and mix well. Pour batter into the prepared muffin pan and bake for 15 minutes. Serve.

Jalapeno Bread

Cook time: 15 minutes | Serves: 4 | Per Serving: Calories 250, Carbs 3g, Fat 22g, Protein 11g

Ingredients:

- Eggs – 4
- Jalapeno chilies – 4, chopped
- Baking powder – 1/4 tsp.
- Coconut flour – 1/3 cup
- Cheddar cheese – 1/2 cup, grated
- Parmesan cheese – 1/4 cup, grated
- Pepper – 1/2 tsp.
- Garlic powder – 1/2 tsp.

- Water – 1/4 cup
- Butter – 1/4 cup
- Salt – 1/2 tsp.

Directions:

Preheat the oven to 400 F. In a bowl, whisk together eggs, pepper, salt, water, and butter. Add baking powder, garlic powder, and coconut flour and mix until well combined. Add jalapenos, cheddar cheese, and parmesan cheese. Mix well and season with pepper. Line baking tray with parchment pepper. Pour batter into a baking tray and bake for 15 minutes. Slices and serve.

Banana Zucchini Bread

Cook time: 45 minutes | Serves: 12 | Per Serving: Calories 78, Carbs 4.4g, Fat 5.8g, Protein 3.4g

Ingredients:

- Eggs – 4
- Cinnamon – 1 tbsp.
- Baking soda – 3/4 tsp.
- Coconut flour – 1/2 cup
- Coconut oil – 1 tbsp.
- Banana – 1, mashed
- Stevia – 1 tsp.
- Zucchini – 1 cup, shredded and squeezed out all liquid
- Walnuts – 1/2 cup, chopped
- Apple cider vinegar – 1 tsp.
- Nutmeg – 1/2 tsp.
- Salt – 1/2 tsp.

Directions:

Preheat the oven to 350 F. Grease loaf pan with oil and set aside. In a large bowl, whisk together egg, banana, oil, and stevia. Add all dry ingredients, vinegar, and zucchini and stir until smooth. Add walnuts and stir well. Pour batter into the loaf pan and bake for 45 minutes. Slice and serve.

Broccoli Bread

Cook time: 30 minutes | Serves: 5 | Per Serving: Calories 205, Carbs 8g, Fat 13g, Protein 13g

Ingredients:

- Eggs – 5, lightly beaten
- Broccoli florets – 3/4 cup, chopped
- Cheddar cheese – 1 cup, shredded
- Baking powder – 2 tsps.
- Coconut flour – 3 1/1 tbsps.
- Salt – 1 tsp.

Directions:

Preheat the oven to 350 F. Grease loaf pan with butter and set aside. Add all ingredients into the bowl and mix well. Pour egg mixture into the prepared loaf pan and bake for 30 minutes. Slice and serve.

Almond Bread

Cook time: 30 minutes | Serves: 20 | Per Serving: Calories 52, Carbs 1g, Fat 4g, Protein 2g

Ingredients:

- Eggs – 6, separated
- Cream of tartar – 1/4 tsp.
- Baking powder – 3 tsp.
- Butter – 4 tbsps., melted
- Almond flour – 1 1/2 cups
- Salt – 1/4 tsp.

Directions:

Preheat the oven to 375 F. Grease 8*4-inch loaf pan with butter and set aside. Add egg whites and cream of tartar in a large bowl and beat until soft peaks form. Add almond flour, baking powder, egg yolks, butter, and salt in a food processor and process until combined. Add 1/3 of egg white mixture into the almond flour mixture and process until combined. Now add remaining egg white mixture and process gently to combine. Pour batter into the prepared loaf pan and bake for 30 minutes. Slice and serve.

Sandwich Bread

Cook time: 50 minutes | Serves: 12 | Per Serving: Calories 125, Carbs 2.5g, Fat 11.5g, Protein 4.7g

Ingredients:

- Coconut flour – 1/2 cup
- Apple cider vinegar – 1 tsp.
- Water – 3/4 cup
- Olive oil – 4 tbsps.
- Eggs – 5
- Baking soda – 1 tsp
- Almond flour – 2 cups + 2 tbsps.
- Salt – 1/2 tsp

Directions:

Preheat the oven to 350 F. Grease loaf pan and set aside. In a large bowl, combine together almond flour, baking soda, coconut flour, and salt. Set aside. Beat eggs in another bowl until frothy. Add vinegar, water, and oil in egg mixture and process until well combined. Add all dry ingredients and process until smooth. Pour batter into the prepared loaf pan and bake for 50 minutes. Slice and serve.

Herb Bread

Cook time: 1 hour 20 minutes | Serves: 12 | Per Serving: Calories 180, Carbs 7g, Fat 12g, Protein 8g

Ingredients:

- Flax-seed meal – 1 cup
- Coconut flour – 1 cup
- Apple cider vinegar – 2 1/2 tbsps.
- Almond milk – 1/2 cup
- Olive oil – 1 1/2 tbsps.
- Eggs – 12
- Garlic powder – 2 tsps.
- Thyme leaves – 1 1/2 tsps., dried
- Sage leaves – 1 tbsp., dried
- Rosemary leaves – 2 tbsps., dried and crumbled
- Baking powder – 4 tsps.
- Whole psyllium husk flakes – 4 tbsps.
- Kosher salt – 1 1/2 tsps.

Directions:

Preheat the oven to 325 F. Grease loaf pan and set aside. In a large bowl, whisk together garlic powder, herbs, salt, baking powder, psyllium husk flakes, flax-seed meal, and coconut flour. Set aside. In a separate large bowl beat eggs until frothy. Add apple cider vinegar, almond milk, and oil into the egg and beat until combined. Slowly add dry ingredients and beat until just combined. Pour batter into the prepared loaf pan and bake for 80 minutes. Slice and serve.

Flax Seed Almond Bread

Cook time: 45 minutes | Serves: 8 | Per Serving: Calories 175, Carbs 7g, Fat 14g, Protein 8.6g

Ingredients:

- Eggs – 4
- Apple cider vinegar – 1/2 tsp.
- Stevia – 2 tsps.
- Baking soda – 1/2 tsp.
- Sea salt – 1/2 tsp.
- Flax seeds – 1 tbsp.
- Ground flax seeds – 1/4 cup
- Almond flour – 1 1/2 cups

Directions:

Preheat the oven to 300 F. Grease loaf pan and set aside. Add all ingredients into the bowl and beat until combined. Pour batter into the prepared loaf pan and bake for 45 minutes. Slice and serve.

Cranberry Bread Loaf

Cook time: 30 minutes | Serves: 10 | Per Serving: Calories 50, Carbs 1.9g, Fat 4g, Protein 1.4g

Ingredients:

- Egg – 1
- Egg whites – 2
- Cranberries – 3 tbsps., chopped
- Baking soda – 1/2 tsp.
- Cinnamon – 1/2 tbsp.
- Cassava flour – 1/3 cup
- Vanilla – 1 tsp.
- Apple cider vinegar – 1/2 tbsp.
- Stevia – 1 tsp.
- Butter – 3 tbsps., melted
- Salt – 1/4 tsp.

Directions:

Preheat the oven to 350 F. Grease loaf pan and set aside. In a bowl, whisk egg whites and egg. Add vanilla, vinegar, and butter. Mix well. Add cranberries, salt, stevia, baking soda, cinnamon, and cassava flour. Mix well. Pour batter into the loaf pan and bake for 30 minutes. Slice and serve.

Chocolate Chip Bread

Cook time: 40 minutes | Serves: 12 | Per Serving: Calories 100, Carbs 8g, Fat 6g, Protein 2g

Ingredients:

- Eggs – 3
- Bananas – 3, mashed
- Chocolate chips – 1/8 cup
- Sea salt – 1/4 tsp.
- Cinnamon – 1/2 tsp.
- Baking soda – 1/2 tsp.
- Baking powder – 1/2 tsp.
- Coconut flour – 1/4 cup
- Vanilla – 1 1/2 tsp.
- Coconut oil – 1/4 cup, melted
- Almond butter – 1/2 cup

Directions:

Preheat the oven to 350 F. Grease loaf pan and set aside. In a large bowl, combine together bananas, vanilla, coconut oil, almond butter, and eggs. Add all dry ingredients and mix well to combine. Pour batter into the prepared loaf pan and bake for 40 minutes. Slice and serve.

Chocolate Muffins

Cook time: 25 minutes | Serves: 9 | Per Serving: Calories 192, Carbs 26g, Fat 9g, Protein 2g

Ingredients:

- Egg – 1
- Chocolate chips – 1/2 cup
- Grape-seed oil – 1/4 cup
- Brewed coffee – 1/2 cup
- Milk – 1/2 cup
- Brown sugar – 1/2 cup
- Sugar – 1/2 cup
- Cocoa powder – 2 tbsps.
- Baking soda – 1/2 tsp.
- Baking powder – 2 tsps.

Directions:

Preheat the oven to 350 F. In a bowl, mix together flour, cocoa powder, baking soda, and baking powder. In a mixing bowl, whisk egg, vanilla, milk, oil, brown sugar, coffee, and sugar until smooth. Add flour mixture and chocolate chips into the egg mixture and fold well. Pour batter into the nine silicone muffin molds and bake for 25 minutes. Serve.

Cinnamon Cranberry Muffins

Cook time: 30 minutes | Serves: 6 | Per Serving: Calories 218, Carbs 17g, Fat 16g, Protein 8g

Ingredients:

- Eggs – 2
- Cranberries – 1/2 cup
- Cinnamon – 1/4 tsp.
- Baking powder – 1 tsp.
- Swerve – 1/4 cup
- Almond flour – 1 1/2 cups
- Vanilla – 1 tsp.
- Sour cream – 1/4 cup
- Pinch of salt

Directions:

Preheat the oven to 325 F. In a bowl, beat sour cream, vanilla, and eggs. Add remaining ingredients except for cranberries and beat until smooth. Add cranberries and stir well. Pour batter into the 6 silicone muffin molds and bake for 25-30 minutes. Serve.

Moist Chocó Muffins

Cook time: 20 minutes | Serves: 9 | Per Serving: Calories 435, Carbs 59g, Fat 19g, Protein 7g

Ingredients:

- Egg – 1
- Canola oil – 1/2 cup
- Vanilla – 1 tsp.
- Milk – 1/2 cup
- Yogurt – 1 cup
- Baking soda – 1 tsp.
- Cocoa powder – 1/2 cup
- Chocolate chips – 1 cup
- Sugar – 1 cup
- All-purpose flour – 2 cups

Directions:

In a large bowl, mix together flour, baking soda, cocoa powder, chocolate chips, and sugar. In a mixing bowl, whisk egg with oil, vanilla, milk, and yogurt until smooth. Add flour mixture into the egg mixture and mix until well combined. Pour batter into the 9 silicone muffin molds and bake at 400 F for 20 minutes. Serve.

Delicious Raspberry Muffins

Cook time: 35 minutes | Serves: 6 | Per Serving: Calories 225, Carbs 13g, Fat 17g, Protein 7g

Ingredients:

- Eggs – 2
- Coconut oil – 2 tbsps.
- Honey – 2 tbsps.
- Raspberries – 3.5 oz.
- Baking powder – 1 tsp.
- Almond meal – 5 oz.

Directions:

Preheat the oven to 350 F. In a medium bowl, mix together almond meal and baking powder. Add honey, eggs, and oil and stir until well combined. Add raspberries and fold well. Spoon batter into the 6 silicone muffin molds and bake for 35 minutes. Serve.

Lemon Blueberry Muffins

Cook time: 20 minutes | Serves: 9 | Per Serving: Calories 345, Carbs 50g, Fat 13g, Protein 6g

Ingredients:

- Eggs – 2
- Blueberries – 1 1/2 cups
- Fresh lemon juice – 2 tsps.
- Lemon zest – 2 tbsps., grated
- Vanilla – 1 tsp.
- Oil – 1/2 cup
- Yogurt – 1 cup
- Sugar – 1 cup
- Baking powder – 1 tbsp.
- Flour – 2 cups
- Salt – 1/2 tsp.

Directions:

Preheat the oven to 375 F. In a small bowl, mix together flour, salt, and baking powder. Set aside. In a large bowl, whisk together eggs, lemon juice, lemon zest, vanilla, oil, yogurt, and sugar. Add flour mixture and blueberries into the egg mixture and mix until combined. Spoon batter into the 9 silicone muffin molds and bake for 20 minutes. Serve.

Moist Banana Bread

Cook time: 35 minutes | Serves: 8 | Per Serving: Calories 240, Carbs 29g, Fat 13g, Protein 4g

Ingredients:

- Egg – 1
- All-purpose flour – 3/4 cup
- Walnuts – 1/2 cup, chopped
- Vanilla – 1/2 tsp.
- Sour cream – 1/4 cup
- Olive oil – 1/4 cup
- Sugar – 1/2 cup
- Ripe bananas – 2
- Baking soda – 1/4 tsp.
- Pinch of salt

Directions:

Grease air fryer baking pan and set aside. In a large bowl, mix together all-purpose flour, baking soda, and salt. Add bananas into the mixing bowl and mash with a fork. Add sugar, egg, vanilla, sour cream, and oil and whisk until smooth. Add flour mixture into the banana mixture and mix until well combined. Add walnuts and stir well. Pour batter into the prepared pan. Place pan in the air fryer basket and bake at 310 F for 35 minutes. Slice and serve.

Drinks

Healthy Strawberry Banana Smoothie

Cook time: 5 minutes | Serves: 1 | Per Serving: Calories 195, Carbs 43g, Fat 0.8g, Protein 6.3g

Ingredients:

- Almond milk – ½ cup
- Banana – 1
- Strawberries – 1 cup

Directions:

Add all ingredients into the blender and blend until smooth and creamy. Serve.

High Protein Strawberry Cheese Smoothie

Cook time: 5 minutes | Serves: 2 | Per Serving: Calories 160, Carbs 22g, Fat 2.5g, Protein 12.4g

Ingredients:

- Cottage cheese – ½ cup
- Vanilla – ¼ tsp.
- Honey – 1 tbsp.
- Strawberries – 1 cup
- Almond milk – 1 cup

Directions:

Add all ingredients into the blender and blend until smooth and creamy. Serve.

Delicious Chocolate Smoothie

Cook time: 5 minutes | Serves: 2 | Per Serving: Calories 145, Carbs 8g, Fat 13g, Protein 4g

Ingredients:

- Almond butter – 4 tbsps.
- Cocoa powder – 4 tbsps.
- Can coconut milk – ½ cup
- Almond milk – 1 cup

Directions:

Add all ingredients into the blender and blend until smooth and creamy. Serve.

Creamy Hot Chocolate

Cook time: 5 minutes | Serves: 4 | Per Serving: Calories 322, Carbs 40g, Fat 12g, Protein 9g

Ingredients:

- Milk – 4 cups
- Vanilla – ¼ tsp.
- Chocolate chips – ½ cup
- Sugar – ¼ cup
- Unsweetened cocoa powder – ¼ cup

Directions:

Add milk, sugar, and cocoa powder in a small saucepan and heat over medium heat. Stir frequently until warm. Add chocolate chips and stir constantly until chocolate chips melt. Stir in vanilla. Serve hot.

Spinach Smoothie

Cook time: 5 minutes | Serves: 1 | Per Serving: Calories 160, Carbs 26g, Fat 5g, Protein 4g

Ingredients:

- Fresh spinach – 2 cups
- Flax seeds – 1 tsp.
- Chia seeds – 1 tsp.
- Fresh turmeric – 1/2-inch piece, peeled and sliced
- Fresh ginger – 1/2-inch piece, peeled and sliced
- Banana – 1/2, cut into slices
- Unsweetened almond milk – 1 cup

Directions:

Add all ingredients into the blender and blend until smooth and creamy. Serve.

Healthy Turmeric Smoothie

Cook time: 5 minutes | Serves: 2 | Per Serving: Calories 413, Carbs 33g, Fat 32g, Protein 4g

Ingredients:

- Turmeric – 1/2 tsp.
- Chia seeds – 1 tsp.
- Ginger – 1/2 tsp.
- Cinnamon – 1/2 tsp.
- Coconut oil – 1 tbsp.
- Banana – 1
- Frozen mango pieces – 1/2 cup
- Hemp milk – 1 cup

Directions:

Add all ingredients into the blender and blend until smooth and creamy. Serve.

Berry Smoothie

Cook time: 5 minutes | Serves: 1 | Per Serving: Calories 696, Carbs 70g, Fat 49g, Protein 8g

Ingredients:

- Fresh raspberries – 1 cup
- Fresh strawberries – 1 cup
- Honey – 1 tsp.
- Coconut oil – 1 tsp.
- Ground cinnamon – 1/2 tsp.
- Turmeric – 1/2 tsp.
- Almond milk – 3/4 cup
- Banana – 3/4 cup

Directions:

Add all ingredients into the blender and blend until smooth and creamy. Serve.

Spinach Cucumber Smoothie

Cook time: 5 minutes | Serves: 1 | Per Serving: Calories 177, Carbs 46g, Fat 0.7g, Protein 2.5g

Ingredients:

- Cucumber – 1/2
- Spinach – 1 cup
- Medium apple – 1, diced
- Honey – 1 tbsp.
- Water – 1 cup

Directions:

Add all ingredients into the blender and blend until smooth and creamy. Serve.

Blueberry Smoothie

Cook time: 5 minutes | Serves: 2 | Per Serving: Calories 360, Carbs 20, Fat 30g, Protein 5g

Ingredients:

- Ground flax seed – 1 tbsp.
- Blueberries – 1 cup
- Almond milk – 1 cup
- Vanilla yogurt – 4 tbsps.
- Spinach – 1/2 cup

Directions:

Add all ingredients into the blender and blend until smooth and creamy. Serve.

Avocado Smoothie

Cook time: 5 minutes | Serves: 1 | Per Serving: Calories 434, Carbs 23g, Fat 39g, Protein 5g

Ingredients:

- Fresh lime juice – 1
- Avocado – 1
- Water – 1/2 cup
- Fresh cilantro – 1/2 cup
- Cucumber – 1/2
- Salt – 1/8 tsp.

Directions:

Add all ingredients into the blender and blend until smooth and creamy. Serve.

Desserts

Classic Yogurt Cake

Cook time: 35 minutes │ Serves: 12 │ Per Serving: Calories 235, Carbs 42g, Fat 6g, Protein 4g

Ingredients:

- Eggs – 2
- Oil – ¼ cup
- Sugar – 7 oz.
- All-purpose flour – 7 oz
- Baking powder – 2 tsps.
- Yogurt – 8.5 oz.

Directions:

In a large bowl, add yogurt, oil, eggs, sugar, flour, and baking powder and mix using a hand mixer until smooth. Preheat the oven to 350 F. Grease a cake pan with butter. Pour cake batter in a prepared pan and bake in a preheated oven for 30-35 minutes. Slice and serve.

Perfect & Easy Brownies

Cook time: 25 minutes │ Serves: 16 │ Per Serving: Calories 202, Carbs 25g, Fat 11.5g, Protein 2.3g

Ingredients:

- Eggs – 3
- Baking powder – ¼ tsp + 1/8 tsp
- Cocoa powder – ½ cup
- Flour – ¾ cup
- Vanilla – 1 ½ tsps.
- Sugar – 1 ½ cups
- Vegetable oil – ¾ cup
- Salt – ¼ tsp.

Directions:

Preheat the oven to 350 F. Grease 9*9-inch baking dish and line with parchment paper and set aside. In a bowl, mix together oil, vanilla, and sugar. Add eggs and whisk until well combined. In a separate bowl, mix together flour, baking powder, cocoa powder, and salt. Slowly add flour mixture to the egg mixture and mix until well combined. Pour batter into the prepared baking dish and bake in preheated oven for 25-30 minutes. Slice and serve.

Choco Lava Cake

Cook time: 1 minute │ Serves: 1 │ Per Serving: Calories 235, Carbs 5.6g, Fat 21.8g, Protein 4.1g

Ingredients:

- Egg yolk – 1
- Chocolate chips – ½ tbsp.
- Vanilla – ¼ tsp.
- Coconut oil – 1 tbsp., melted
- Coconut milk – ¼ cup
- Baking powder – ¼ tsp.
- Stevia – 2 tbsps.
- Cocoa powder – 2 tbsps.
- Almond flour – 3 tbsps.
- Pinch of salt

Directions:

In a bowl, mix together flour, baking powder, stevia, cocoa powder, and salt. Add milk, vanilla, oil, and egg yolk and stir until well combined. Spray mug with cooking spray and pour batter in mug. Place mug in microwave and microwave for 50-60 seconds on high. Let it sit for 1-2 minutes. Serve.

Classic Chocolate Fudge

Cook time: 10 minutes | Serves: 25 | Per Serving: Calories 145, Carbs 12g, Fat 9g, Protein 2g

Ingredients:

- Semisweet chocolate chips – 2 cups
- Walnuts – 1 cup, chopped
- Vanilla – 2 tsps.
- Sweetened condensed milk – ½ cup
- Bittersweet chocolate – 2 oz

Directions:

Line 8-inch baking dish with wax paper and set aside. Add bittersweet chocolate, condensed milk, and chocolate chips into the double boiler and stir until chocolate is melted. Stir in walnuts and vanilla. Spread fudge mixture into the prepared baking dish and place in the refrigerator for 2 hours or until firm. Slice and serve.

Coconut Chocolate Pops

Cook time: 5 minutes | Serves: 8 | Per Serving: Calories 123, Carbs 7g, Fat 11g, Protein 1.7g

Ingredients:

- Can coconut milk – 14 oz.
- Vanilla – 1 tsp.
- Honey – 2 tbsps.
- Cocoa powder – 1/3 cup
- Pinch of kosher salt

Directions:

Add all ingredients into the blender and blend for minute. Pour blended mixture into the popsicles molds and place in the refrigerator for 4-5 hours or until set. Serve.

Chewy Chocolate Brownies

Cook time: 20 minutes | Serves: 16 | Per Serving: Calories 150, Carbs 21g, Fat 7g, Protein 1.4g

Ingredients:

- All-purpose flour – 1 1/3 cups
- Vanilla – ½ tsp.
- Vegetable oil – ½ cup
- Water – ½ cup
- Baking powder – ½ tsp.
- Cocoa powder – 1/3 cup
- Sugar – 1 cup
- Salt – ½ tsp.

Directions:

Grease 8*8-inch baking pan and set aside. In a large mixing bowl, mix together flour, baking powder, cocoa powder, sugar, and salt. In a small bowl, whisk together oil, water, and vanilla. Pour oil mixture into the flour mixture and mix until combined. Pour batter into the prepared pan and bake at 350 F for 20 minutes. Slice and serve.

Strawberry Cobbler

Cook time: 45 minutes | Serves: 6 | Per Serving: Calories 390, Carbs 60g, Fat 16g, Protein 2g

Ingredients:

- Strawberries – 2 cups, diced
- Vanilla – 1 tsp.
- Butter – ½ cup, melted
- Unsweetened almond milk – 1 cup
- Self-raising flour – 1 cup
- Sugar – 1 ¼ cup

Directions:

Preheat the oven to 350 F. Grease 11*8-inch baking dish and set aside. In a bowl, mix together flour and 1 cup sugar. Add milk and whisk until smooth. Add vanilla and butter and mix well. Pour mixture into the prepared dish and sprinkle with strawberries and top with remaining sugar. Bake for 45 minutes. Serve.

Blueberry Popsicles

Cook time: 5 minutes | Serves: 8 | Per Serving: Calories 64, Carbs 16g, Fat 0.2g, Protein 0.5g

Ingredients:

- Frozen blueberries – 3 cups
- Honey – ¼ cup
- Lemon juice – 2 tbsps.

Directions:

Add all ingredients into the blender and blend until smooth. Pour blended mixture into the Popsicle molds and place in the fridge 4-6 hours or until set. Serve.

Silky Mango Mousse

Cook time: 10 minutes | Serves: 2 | Per Serving: Calories 328, Carbs 57g, Fat 12g, Protein 3g

Ingredients:

- Mangoes – 2, chopped
- Sugar – 1 tbsp.
- Heavy whipping cream – ½ cup

Directions:

Add mangoes and sugar into the blender and blend until smooth. Add heavy whipping cream into the large bowl and beat until smooth. Add blended mango mixture and mix well. Pour into the serving glasses and place in the fridge for 30 minutes. Serve.

Delicious Peanut Butter Cake

Cook time: 30 minutes | Serves: 9 | Per Serving: Calories 280, Carbs 40g, Fat 10g, Protein 9g

Ingredients:

- All-purpose flour – 1 ½ cups
- Vegetable oil – 1/3 cup
- Baking soda – 1 tsp.
- Peanut butter powder – ½ cup
- Sugar – 1 cup
- Vanilla – 1 tsp.
- Apple cider vinegar – 1 tbsp.
- Water – 1 cup
- Salt – ½ tsp.

Directions:

Preheat the oven to 350 F. Grease cake pan and set aside. In a large mixing bowl, mix together flour, baking soda, peanut butter powder, sugar, and salt. In a small bowl, whisk together oil, vanilla, vinegar, and water. Pour oil mixture into the flour mixture and stir to combine. Pour batter into the prepared pan and bake for 30 minutes. Allow to cool for 10-15 minutes. Slice and serve.

Easy Peanut Butter Fudge

Cook time: 10 minutes | Serves: 25 | Per Serving: Calories 105, Carbs 7g, Fat 7g, Protein 3g

Ingredients:

- Peanut butter – 1 ¼ cups
- Coconut milk – ½ cup
- Sugar – ¼ cup
- Maple syrup – 1/3 cup
- Pinch of salt

Directions:

Line 8*8-inch baking pan with parchment paper and set aside. Add all ingredients into the saucepan and heat over medium heat. Whisk until oil is melted and everything is well combined. Pour mixture into the prepared baking pan and place in the refrigerator until set, about 2 hours. Slice and serve.

Baked Apple Slices

Cook time: 30 minutes | Serves: 2 | Per Serving: Calories 128, Carbs 24g, Fat 4g, Protein 0.3g

Ingredients:

- Butter – 2 tbsps.
- Apples – 2, peeled, cored, and sliced
- Cinnamon – 1 tsp.
- Sugar – ¼ cup
- Brown sugar – ¼ cup
- Salt – ¼ tsp.

Directions:

Preheat the oven to 350 F. Grease 9-inch baking dish and set aside. Add cinnamon, sugar, brown sugar, and salt into the zip-lock bag and mix well. Add apple slices into the bag and shake until well coated. Add apple slices into the prepared baking dish and bake for 25-30 minutes. Serve.

Chia Chocó Pudding

Cook time: 10 minutes | Serves: 3 | Per Serving: Calories 245, Carbs 50g, Fat 5g, Protein 6g

Ingredients:

- Can full-fat coconut milk – 14 oz.
- Vanilla – 1 tsp.
- Chia seeds – ¼ cup
- Maple syrup – ½ cup
- Cocoa powder – ½ cup
- Salt – 3/8 tsp.

Directions:

Add all ingredients into the blender and blend until smooth. Pour blended mixture into the serving cups and place in the fridge for 4-6 hours. Serve.

Lemon Blueberry Sorbet

Cook time: 5 minutes | Serves: 1 | Per Serving: Calories 135, Carbs 33g, Fat 0.8g, Protein 1.5g

Ingredients:

- Frozen blueberries – 7 oz.
- Maple syrup – 1 tsp.
- Fresh lemon juice – 1 tbsp.

Directions:

Add all ingredients into the blender and blend until smooth. Pour blended mixture into the air-tight container and place in the fridge until firm. Serve.

Choco Cashew Butter Fudge

Cook time: 10 minutes | Serves: 10 | Per Serving: Calories 249, Carbs 6g, Fat 23g, Protein 4g

Ingredients:

- Cashew butter – ½ cup
- Unsweetened chocolate chips – ½ cup
- Coconut oil – ½ cup

Directions:

Line 9*5-inch loaf pan with parchment paper and set aside. Add all ingredients into the double boiler on medium heat until melted. Stir well. Pour melted mixture into the prepared pan and place in the fridge until set. Slice and serve.

Conclusion

A vegetarian diet is a healthy eating choice that encourages you to eat fresh and healthy plant-based foods. Compare to non-vegetarian food, vegetarian foods are high in fiber content and also lower in cholesterol and saturated fats. A study published by the University of Oxford in January 2013 in the American Journal of Clinical Nutrition Scientific research shows that people who follow a vegetarian diet have a lower risk of heart disease, diabetes, obesity, osteoporosis, and in some cases it reduced the risk of cancer, compared to non-vegetarians. The book contains 250 different types of authentic, healthy, delicious, and tasty recipes. All the recipes are written in this book are easily understandable and made from simple ingredients which are easily available in your kitchen. All the recipes come with their exact preparation time, cooking and their exact nutritional values.

Printed in Great Britain
by Amazon